Drama and Theatre
in Education

Drama and Theatre in Education

Edited by

NIGEL DODD

and

WINIFRED HICKSON

HEINEMANN
LONDON

Heinemann Educational Books Ltd
LONDON EDINBURGH MELBOURNE
TORONTO NEW DELHI AUCKLAND
SINGAPORE JOHANNESBURG HONG KONG
NAIROBI IBADAN

ISBN 0 435 18270 6

Published by Heinemann Educational Books Ltd
48 Charles Street, London W1X 8AH
Printed in Great Britain by Cox & Wyman Ltd
London, Fakenham and Reading

Contents

What needs to be done is not to define the frontiers of a subject where no frontiers exist, but to establish clearly the contribution of dramatic activity to the growth and education of children.

Drama: Education Survey 2
Department of Education and Science

Foreword

THIS CONFERENCE resulted from the admirable collaboration of a local education authority, a professional theatre, and an independent school. It established clearly that interest in drama is widespread and goes 'right across the board'; and that this interest involves many aspects of current educational thinking. The formal contributions in the earlier part of this book testify to the quality of thought that is being given to drama; the ranging discussions in the latter part to its breadth. We have here enough unanswered questions to keep us going for many years. I look back on the Clifton Conference with gratitude to its organizers for three days of exhilarating meetings and discussions. Colley Cibber in his Autobiography says, 'Could HOW Betterton spoke be as easily known as WHAT he spoke; then might you see the muse of Shakespeare in her triumph.' If readers can fill in behind the printed words on the following pages something of the humour, the eruptions of passion, the swift disagreements, the excitement at a moment of penetration, then they will get an idea of whatever is meant by drama at its most stimulating and persuasive.

JOHN ALLEN

PART ONE

Introduction

THE ORIGIN of this book was a conference on 'Drama and Theatre in Education' held at Clifton College from Monday 31 March to Thursday 3 April 1969, sponsored by the Bristol Education Authority, the Bristol Old Vic Theatre Company, and Clifton College, which was designed as a follow-up to the Department of Education and Science Drama Survey and aimed to look critically at the various kinds of activity embraced by 'Drama and Theatre in Education' and the claims made for them. The conference, which was heavily over-subscribed, was attended by 330 people representing infant, primary, secondary, college of education and university levels – in addition there were some fifteen drama advisers, and representatives from theatres and theatre in education groups including Billingham, Bolton, Bristol, Cheltenham, Coventry, Salisbury and Watford.

The plan was to open the conference with a survey of current practice and thinking and to devote the second day to the presentation of a variety of approaches through demonstration and description. The first part of this book consists of a record of these talks and presentations modified for reading and, in the case of the paper on Movement for Drama by Veronica Sherborne, specially written, as the main part of her original contribution took the form of a demonstration.

Gavin Bolton's paper wittily surveys some recent attitudes to drama and the other contributors explore specific themes or special emphases: John Hodgson shows how literature can be understood more deeply through improvisation and how improvisation can be enriched by literature; Dorothy Heathcote, while emphasizing the importance of understanding the needs of the children and the nature of drama, argues that the teacher needs to understand himself, particularly his strengths, more fully; Veronica Sherborne describes the importance of a rich movement vocabulary in developing awareness in the teachers of normal and

handicapped children, and in drama student, alike; John Hersee
sees the school play as in no way opposed to educational drama,
and stresses the variety of skills and talents required and the sheer
enjoyment of a challenge which provides a special opportunity
for the gifted and enthusiastic to join in a unifying extra-curricular
activity; the conference also saw *Guns*,[1] an improvised revue-
style play based on the assassination of Robert Kennedy, devised
and performed by some Sixth Formers of Lawrence Weston
School, a Bristol Comprehensive School, which threw into
relief the whole question of how far and how soon improvised
work in drama ought to be developed into audience-orientated
theatre.

The account of current approaches of some professional
theatres working in the educational field is by Mark Woolgar,
Staff Producer with the Bristol Old Vic Company. He questions
the depth and effectiveness of some work and stresses the importance of co-operation between theatres and teachers and the
need for financial stability if clear aims and purposes are to be
backed by long-term planning. The conference was fortunate to
experience some of the methods of the work by the 'Theatre in
Education' team of the Belgrade Theatre, Coventry, and to hear
something of what was being done in a situation where thoughtful
planning was combined with close liaison between theatre and
schools and backed by generous grants.

The intention was that the talks and demonstrations would
provide a common experience and help to sharpen the discussion
which took place in small groups on the Wednesday and Thursday
mornings of the conference. The aim of the discussions on
Wednesday was to try to see the place of Drama and Theatre in
the total picture of the educational situation and of the educational
needs of children; the aim of the discussion on Thursday was for
each group to explore one aspect of the subject more fully. In
order to help these discussions a number of interested teachers,
educationists and people concerned with the professional
theatre had a series of meetings before the conference and produced discussion papers on some central areas and on a wide
variety of more specialized topics.[2] The reports of the general

[1] Appendix III provides a brief description of *Guns* by the Sixth Former
who was chiefly concerned with its production.

[2] These discussion papers and preliminary theme papers by most of the
'presenters' will be found in Appendix II.

and particular discussions by the various groups of the conference forms the second part of this book.

We should like to thank all those who so warmly supported the conference.

Bristol, 1970   NIGEL DODD
                                              WINIFRED HICKSON

1. Drama and Theatre in Education: a survey

Gavin Bolton

THE PROSPECT of preparing a survey of educational drama and theatre in this country has alarmed me. Although by the nature of my job I am in a privileged position that allows me to see a great deal of drama teaching in many parts of the country, anything I do by way of formal assessment would fall far short of the admirable document published by the Department of Education and Science two years ago.

So I discounted the idea of a survey and decided that what I ought to do was perhaps to present a very seriously-minded paper on some aspect of drama in education, but when I looked at the programme for this conference I realized that those attending were already getting that kind of meat – in fact five meat courses. I wondered if I might miss out the soup and just treat this essay as the *hors d'œuvre*.

One admirable quality of the D.E.S. report was that it was objective, utterly reasonable in tone and fair-minded in its comments. I should like to be utterly subjective, unreasonable in tone and quite biased in comment.

In the blurb that was sent out to us about this conference, it says quite firmly, 'it is appreciated that no final answers should be given to questions that this conference will be considering'. One appreciates that if there is to be any advance at all in any area – philosophy and science or the arts – the advance takes place when somebody asks a new question, but it is an unfortunate feature of our profession that the practitioner in the classroom is never in a position to ask questions because, faced with thirty expectant faces, he must know (or think he knows) the answer; and because he is usually desperately short of time and generally wrung dry by the end of a week, he depends on the answers other people have cooked up for him.

Such has been my career. My thirteen years of teaching in schools seems to have been measured out by whatever educational theories (sometimes half-digested) I happened to have bumped into at any one stage. I suppose it can be divided nicely into three phases. The first phase is called 'The Play's the Thing'; the second phase is called 'The Play is certainly not the thing' and the third phase (which is now) is called 'The Play's the Thing'. All I seem to have done is to get back to where I started – with a significant difference.

I propose, therefore, to be somewhat autobiographical, not because there has been something special about my career, but rather the reverse; I suspect that many teachers will find their own experience outlined in mine so that although I am avoiding doing the kind of survey implied in the title my personal account may indeed reflect the many kinds of activities that function under the name of drama in this country today.

A testimonial on leaving college suggested that my talents for acting and play production would prove to be very useful skills in the promotion of drama work in school. This view concurred with my own. Teaching in a Primary School, I applied these skills at every opportunity, in spite of the obvious handicap of not having a hall with a stage. However, a local hall could be hired for the bi-annual occasion of the school concert so that children would have the full-blooded experience of footlights, stage-sets (box and/or pantomime varieties) and a packed house.

By comparison, the classroom drama done in between productions fell a long way short of the ideal. However, we did our best by giving the children (the best readers I'm talking about of course) a fairly wide range of characters to act from various publications of nice little plays for nice little people and then training them to understand that as the front of the classroom represented 'on-stage' anyone standing by the windows or by the door was off-stage right and left respectively and my role as producer was to sit at the back of the classroom (a dual function here of keeping an eye on the fidgety spectators) giving constructive advice like, 'I can't hear you' or 'You're slow on your cue' or 'No, say it this way, dear'.

Pleasant as this was for me and for the actors, drama lessons were marred by the growing lack of attention of the audience, so

I changed tactics. I had for some time been concerned that in our school productions many children failed to project their voices to the back row of the parish hall. This was allied to the other problem of having a number of children who, although fluent readers, could not be cast in decent parts because of their inexpressive speech.

So drama lessons became speech lessons. (In the meantime I gained for myself a certain Speech and Drama Diploma qualification that had very little to do with the teaching of drama but a great deal to do with professional promotion to drama posts.) All the class, relishing every carefully graded consonant and vowel, participated in the hilarious chorus of jingles and tongue-twisters with admirable uniformity. Until I read a book on mime.

It seemed so obvious, once I had read the book, that precision in speech should be matched by precision in bodily movement. And this book was so helpful. It told me how to divide a lesson up so that all the senses were imaginatively activated ('All smell an orange') and every main section of the body duly exercised ('You're great tall trees'). But it also guided me on which exercises were appropriate to different age-groups. Not that I kept rigidly to the set text – threading needles for example seemed popular with all ages. And it was all so peaceful.

Thus for me a pattern for the teaching of drama to primary school children had emerged – speech and mime practice culminating in the climactic experience of presenting plays to an adult audience. Life seemed well ordered. Until I attended a course of lectures.

It was supposed to be about how to teach drama – but the speakers kept talking about the child. Apparently the child had his own kind of drama, if only teachers would give him a chance. This was a revelation and pretty unpalatable. The advocates of this child-centred philosophy talked of drama in terms of developmental growth, or natural rhythms and of spontaneous expression, and of the teacher as an observer, as a follower. But in fact they were asking me as a trained teacher of some three or four years' experience to unlearn the very skills that had made me a good teacher. I had seen myself as an interpreter of texts, as a manipulator of children towards artistic standards, as a trainer in speech and mime. Now I was being asked to abdicate from all this in favour of freedom of expression. Theatre and scripts were now dirty words.

It was during my post in a Secondary Modern School as teacher of English, Drama and Maths that I first tried the new drama. I made the mistake, committed by many impressionable young teachers who are anxious to absorb the latest methods, of abandoning all I knew from my own experience and allowing myself to be taken over by what I understood of the new principles. In practice, therefore, I conveyed to my classes that the drama session was theirs and that they should get on with it. They did.

As the volume of sound rose above permissible metal-work class noise-level the headmaster's distressed eyebrows would appear over the pane of glass in the door. It was some time before he challenged me openly about my creative drama work. He appeared to be more than satisfied with the successful rigidity of my school play production and the silent formality of my maths teaching (it did not occur to me at that time that the philosophy I was attempting to acquire was not just applicable to drama but should form the basis of all teaching situations) but what did I think I was doing in drama lessons? My reply was a masterpiece of self-righteous arrogance. I pointed out to him, using my recently acquired tone of spiritual dedication, that form 3A whom we had always regarded as a bright set, co-operative enough under firm treatment, were really misunderstood, emotionally disturbed, deprived adolescents for whom this kind of drama was therapeutic release.

My answer to the headmaster sounded confident enough, but my faith in child-centred drama failed me as I bit my finger-nails through endless sessions of robbing banks, and cowboys and Indians without any apparent change taking place. But when I went on some more courses I discovered that other people who were interested in the 'free' drama hadn't taken it as literally as I had. It didn't simply mean, 'Let them get on with it'. They had all kinds of controls. There are four which I think are most common.

One is called 'take one record' control. With this one you have a record and you work out a sequence of actions to the music and they are controlled by it. Marvellous! The piece that I kept using was from the *Peer Gynt Suite*, 'In the Hall of the Mountain King'. You tell them what the situation is, you tell them what to do to it and then away they go. You have them all as trolls – fast asleep of course; they awaken slowly moving (for some reason no one ever challenges) just one small part of the body, gradually building up to a frenzy of twisting and twirling and reeling and writhing. But you don't worry because you have told them that the three crashes in the movement at the end are three cracks in the roof of the cavern and they are all going to fall down, when the right moment comes, and they all dutifully collapse on the floor ... dead. Splendid! Then they say, 'Can we do it again, sir?' and you say 'Yes,' secure in the knowledge that it will be a pattern repeated.

Another form of control is to send them into their drama groups. I was sold on this idea for a long time, where you begin the lesson 'Right, into your drama groups! Make up a play,' and the teacher either sits down and let's them get on with it or chases round from group to group giving encouragement to almost anything. Even when I was Drama Adviser I used to recommend this to teachers until I realized one day on visiting a school that I was seeing a group of children who were in their same drama corners making up the same kinds of plays they had made up two years earlier.

Another kind of control is to have your list and a tambour. Now with this kind of control you have a sequence of events that you put them through. As the narrator you say 'When I shake this tambour' (you've got to have the right kind of voice for this) 'you slowly will wake up and before you there will be a great mountain' tap the tambour and they all blithely wake up and go up a mountain. 'When you get to the top there is a castle with great gates and I want you to push those gates, P-U-S-H H-A-R-D. Good'. And so it goes on and on and then you might give them a little imaginative touch by saying they go through a door, and may risk something by 'I don't know what there is on the other side ... '

And then the fourth kind of control is possibly the easiest way of doing drama altogether; let the B.B.C. do it. A kind voice comes over the radio and tells you to find a space. This is called 'drama by remote control'.

Having half-absorbed all these methods of doing drama, I was obviously qualified to become a drama adviser. I don't know whether my advice to teachers was of any value, but I always had to preface it with an admission that I needed to learn from them as much as they from me. It was about this time that I learnt of a different approach from anything I had known so far. I went on a Ministry Course. They told me that the way into drama was not through speech, was not through mime, was not through the child, but through movement.

In all my course attending, nothing has brought me as much personal satisfaction and pleasure as this experience in movement. I was very thrilled though I discovered it rather late in my career. I have never been very happy, however, about the theory that movement leads to drama. It seems to me that it leads to everything. I think it is the most basic form of education and will have its effect on maths and science and art and P.E. and dance, writing and drama. It certainly has its effect on drama. But it doesn't naturally lead to it because, as I see it, it tends to work on an abstract plane that moves in an opposite direction from drama.

Now in thinking about all these possible methods (and if you do think about them, surely the aims behind them are contradictory), the emphasis has been on the script, the emphasis has been on speech, on mime, on the child and on movement. But it was never on the thing that is created (unless, of course, scripted work may be said to put the emphasis there but scripted work was not the children's creation, and tended to mean more to me than to the children I taught). And this seems to me to be the problem. What is drama? When is drama, drama? When does educational drama go to the heart of drama? We should be able to ask this question: what is the nature and function of drama when it operates at its highest level of achievement?

It seems to me that possibly an answer to this is, when it is composed of those elements that are common to both children's play and to theatre, when the aims are to help children to learn about those feelings, attitudes and preconceptions that, before the drama was experienced, were too implicit for them to be aware of. This means going to the dramatic situation, to the created play, for drama is concerned, as I see it, with the refining of those concepts to do with inter-personal relationships. There is no escaping from this. It may be that there are times when, for valid educational reasons, we put the emphasis on speech and movement and so on, but I feel we must aim at using the heart of drama, which is the dramatic situation. And our aims are not concerned with developing confidence, developing poise or even, primarily developing a tool of expression. Our aims are helping children to understand, so that (if I may use some phrases from the Farmington Trust Research in another context), they are helped to face facts and to interpret them without prejudice; so that they develop a range and degree of identification with other people; so that they develop a set of principles, a set of consistent principles, by which they are going to live.

I believe that when drama is a group-sharing of a dramatic situation it is more powerful than any other medium in education for achieving the kind of aims that I have listed. But this kind of drama puts tremendous strain, tremendous responsibility on the teacher. He has a very positive role because children left to themselves can only work horizontally at a 'what should happen next' level. It is the teachers' judicious questioning and the timing of that questioning that is going to translate a play about robbing a bank to a play that has 'robbing the bank' as a framework for a challenging theme. It can be about a group of men who are struggling for leadership in a gang. It can be an examination of the quality of living of a man who is a gang member and a family man and a citizen. It can be about each individual's claim to a share of the loot. It can be about the women who are left behind when there is a job on. It can be about what it's like to do a job for which you have got to get 10 out of 10 because $9\frac{1}{2}$ out of 10 is a failure. And it is the teacher and only the teacher, who can dig deep and make a frivolous or a trivial (in the eyes of the adults) suggestion something worth pursuing, something worth getting to grips with, so that there is a deeper understanding of a fundamental human issue. Things that the children have always understood implicitly will come to the surface. It may be that they don't come to the surface as they do it as much as when the teacher asks the question after it is done. They suddenly know that they have learned because they have been allowed to verbalize it, and the verbalization is rooted in the concrete sensory/motor experience of the dramatic action.

Of course, all this, where the teacher is helping to make the drama about something, where cowboys and Indians finishes up with a theme, is very close to what theatre is about. But curiously, young children, and here I am meaning particularly mid-juniors and above, who are quite capable of being intellectually stretched by their drama because they are identifying with it so completely and because the identification takes place when they are on their feet, are not able to derive the same benefits from seeing adult theatre do its equivalent of cops and robbers. The form of identification required is too sophisticated for young children. The physical element is taken out and there is no teacher there prodding, asking the right questions at the right time as the theatre experience takes place. The children in their own drama are experiencing a growth and a process. Theatre is the end product of someone else's process, and drama in schools doesn't concern itself primarily with end-products.

So it seems, therefore, that it doesn't really matter if junior school children never go to the theatre and even secondary children find this process of identification very difficult indeed. But they can be trained. The question is 'who should do the training?' I believe that the right people for training secondary children to appreciate theatre are professional theatre people themselves. I have seen some brilliant lessons to small groups of children given by some young directors in this country. They have the know-how, they have the equipment and they have the actors to demonstrate. So they, I am sure, are potentially more capable than most of us who are teachers. What I do object to very strongly as far as the professional theatre is concerned, are those companies that claim that they know how to train teachers for their classroom work. Indeed one company runs a course for teachers called 'Drama in Schools'. It is very important that we respect each other's professionalism and expertise more. Opportunities need to be created for actors, directors and teachers to meet to learn from each other.

Now there is an interesting aspect of theatre in education, handled over a great number of years by one leading professional company and employed occasionally by a number of experienced amateur/teacher groups, where the educational value is clearly defined and the form of presentation is dictated by an attempt to understand the developmental needs of children. I call this work 'theatre in the classroom'. A number of professional companies are now springing up who offer many different variations of this work where the teaching skill needs to equal the acting skill. It is exciting to note the growing number of professional theatre-in-education people who have teaching qualifications as well as actor training. Critics may be justified in some cases in labelling this zeal for children's theatre as educational band-wagon jumping, and I have seen some pretty dismal, tongue-in-cheek 'we are acting down to children' presentations by one or two professional companies; but generally there is an enlightened and serious attitude to the work and in the last twelve months I have seen some educational theatre projects that have been quite brilliant. If this kind of work is to be extended, could Theatre Schools consider providing a course of training for students attracted to this actor/teacher profession?

As I said at the beginning, my college in no way prepared me for teaching drama, apart from the encouragement it gave to formal play-production. The result has been that until I found the kind of job where I had time and opportunity to hammer out my own philosophy and practice of drama in education, with much more enthusiasm than understanding, I dabbled in all kinds of approaches, half-absorbed from casual short-course or conference contacts. I suspect that a large number of teachers in the profession have shared my experiences.

But now fewer drama enthusiasts entering the profession know as little about educational drama as I did. Indeed, there appears to be a glorious harvest of drama-trained students leaving colleges each summer. (Unfortunately the amount of drama in schools does not correspondingly increase – even the best students cannot always cope with the very real lack of understanding among the rest of the profession.) It is, however, worth while asking the question, 'When a student has been trained in drama, what is the nature of his expertise? And does his contribution to the education of children differ in kind or in skill if he has taken drama at college curriculum level, main course, B.Ed., theatre school, supplementary course, advanced diploma or degree?'

There is not time to attempt an answer to these questions but it seems to me that, whatever kind of training a teacher has had, he should be equipped with the following resources:

(i) He should know how to build mutual trust between himself and his class so that both can reveal feelings, enthusiasms and interests with a large degree of honesty.

(ii) He should have the kind of eye for really seeing what is happening when children are working at their drama, what is happening to the children as persons and also in terms of the drama created.

(iii) Having recognized what is happening at these two levels he should have the skill to help extend the quality of the drama along a direction that is in keeping with what appears to be the educational needs of the children at that particular moment.

How does a graduate in drama who goes into teaching receive training in these fundamental skills? How can the student in a

College of Education acquire more than a few useful how-to-begin exercises in a curriculum crash-course? And what exactly are the priorities of all the other courses in between?

It is the role of a conference like this to ask the questions that will help us define our priorities.

2. Improvisation and Literature

John Hodgson

EVERYBODY, of course, knows what *Literature* is, but few have been foolhardy enough to attempt any kind of delimitation of it. Those who wrote the *Oxford Companion to Literature* did not attempt this task. It is assumed that if you consult the volume you are already aware of what literature is. The *Oxford English Dictionary* is not really much more helpful. 'Literature', the *New English Dictionary* tells us, is 'acquaintance with letters or books, literary culture', whilst 'literary' is recorded as being 'of or pertaining to, or of the nature of literature'/'polite learning, books, or written composition'.

For the purpose of this investigation, I have taken 'literature' to be 'books or written composition' (though not always ' polite') which for a shorter or longer time has received a certain (or uncertain) body of acclaim. It is essentially (and this is an important point) *recorded* or *printed* or *permanent*. It has the quality of being tested, tried and ponderable. Here I have taken a broad view of what is acceptable as literature: you will see that my illustrations go back as far as Aesop and come as close to the present time as John Lennon and Paul McCartney.

Improvisation, though it has been with us for a longer time, is a more difficult word. We may accept this or that piece of literature (and there are many stories, poems and plays that we would accept, all of us, as being part of literature), but agreement is not so easy with regard to improvisation. It is both a younger and an older concept than literature. We do not yet have an agreed volume called *The Oxford Companion to Improvisation*. There are those who will swear by it and say that it is the basis of all drama, while others can give it no tolerance at all. Between them stand those with a range of views, many giving lip-service to the theoretical value of improvisation, though they may well add that they have never actually used it! I think much of this disagreement is not so much about the value as about the meaning of the word. It is both an educational and a dramatic method.

When I was working with the Bristol Old Vic Theatre School, we had a course intended to train young directors, and this included opportunities to watch established directors at work. On one of these occasions we saw Tyrone Guthrie directing rehearsals for *The Alchemist* at the Old Vic in London. The first scene rehearsed in the morning was one the actors had not been through before. Most of them were working with books, and, as often happens when actors (of any age or experience) are being watched in rehearsal, tension began to mount. After a while, Guthrie stopped the action and told the actors to stand at the side of the stage and go through their lines.

Those of us watching were surprised at this method, which seemed to be a kind of recitation. Afterwards, in discussion, one of the young observers asked the great man why he had not used improvisation. Guthrie's reply was 'We never have time for improvisation; I've never used it and I've never found it necessary'.

Now Tyrone Guthrie is a man of the theatre and not an educationist. If he had had any educational training he might have analysed the problem differently. His actors did not *know* enough of what the scene was about, and the solution he chose was repetition. The young director was suggesting investigation. He was recommending the setting up of situations in which the actors would raise questions about relationships and content of the scene and through activity gain insight into its human and dramatic qualities. But it was difficult for discussion to follow because there was no common experience. The young director had discovered some things about improvisation but Guthrie accepted the fact that he had no time for it.

Sometimes when we think we are considering values we are really debating concepts. Before deciding whether a thing works, we have to be sure we know what it is that we are trying to make work. Then we need to try it out in a variety of circumstances before we can fairly pass any judgement about it.

Though we may not adequately be able to define the idea, we must make clear the sense and implications in which we employ it.

Throughout this paper I will be suggesting some of the breadth of meanings of improvisation and here let me lay down some vital elements which are present in all improvisations. It is, 'any expressive response to a stimulus, provided that that expression has some element of spontaneity within it.' Expression might be in purely visual terms, it might be in oral terms, or it may be in a combination of both visual and oral, but there will always be spontaneity. The qualities then, which I see in improvisation, are that it is *responsive*, that it is *shared*, that it is *transient*, *momentary*, even *impulsive*.

So, there are two concepts: on the one hand the idea of literature, as that which is *tried, tested, permanent, fixed, written, reflected;* and on the other hand, the idea of improvisation as that which is *spontaneous, responsive, impermanent, momentary.*

Now if you can see these two ideas as being, as it were, at opposite ends of our expression and understanding, we can begin to appreciate how the two can work together; how, in fact, they can serve each other admirably. I have organized the many possible points of emphasis into three broad groups:

1. Ways in which improvisation can be used to enable us (teachers or students) to introduce literature – a preparatory measure, a means of opening up the ground so that it is possible to be more receptive to themes, stories, and characters in literature.

2. Ways in which improvisation can be used to help us to discover literature. Having prepared our minds for literature, improvisation can be a means of finding out many of its qualities. It can help in re-examining, re-vitalizing, and bringing this which is fixed and permanent and of lasting value into something which is more responsive and immediate, and

3. – this turns the process round – ways in which literature can help us to improve our improvisations and can stimulate the richer development of our drama by suggesting the ideas, the material or the methods.

But first, here are a few other elements which make improvisation at once both a fascinating and a challenging method with which to work:

(a) Improvisation is always going to be infinitely varied
Some time ago I gave students from different parts of the country a copy of the Aesop's fable *The Fox and the Crow*. It was set down like this:

One day the fox was walking by the edge of the forest when he saw the crow sitting high up in a tree with a large piece of cheese in his mouth. The fox was feeling rather hungry, so he began to scheme how to get the crow to give him the cheese. He was sure that flattery was the way, so he began:

'Good morning, Mr Crow, sir, and how are we?'

But the crow didn't even turn his head. Undaunted, the fox continued:

'How handsome you are looking today, the Prince of the Forest, in fact.'

At this, the crow began preening his feathers, which led the fox to turn on even more of his charm.

'I am sure a fine bird such as yourself has a beautiful voice. Please sing to me.'

The crow, wanting to show off his talents, threw back his head and began his violent croaking. Of course, when he opened his mouth he dropped the cheese! The fox snapped it up and ran off into the forest, leaving the crow to his awful croaking.

Each person was asked to read the story and then to retell it, using his local dialect. Here are three of these expressions in response to the stimulus.

The first is a Liverpool version – racy, rapid, neatly shaped and slightly condensing the original. Even on the page it is possible to sense the spontaneity, liveliness and immediacy of the delivery.

Well, anyway, there was this crow like, who fancied himself a bit – you know what I mean – and he had this bit of cheese stuck in his gob. Well, along comes this fox who says, 'I'm starved'. With that the fox sees the crow and the cheese. 'Here's my chance', he says. 'All right there Crow, how's it going'. The crow just looked at the fox as if it was thick, like – 'Eh, handsome, you'll look as if you could go places with a face like yours, you know what I mean'. Still no reaction from the crow. 'Give us a turn there Crow, I'm a talent spotter'. Well, the stupid crow opens his gob and screams out these sort o' notes and of course drops the cheese. 'The gear' says the fox, picking up the cheese with his teeth and making away chuffed to the eyeballs with himself.

Some of the improvisations we see in class will begin with qualities like this. Some will be fast and furious, somewhat inaudible and perhaps concluded in a very short time. We must not be surprised and need to know how to go on from here.

The next version indicates a more leisurely approach, giving the material a slightly different mood and establishing the cockney personality through vocabulary and local phrases as much as through accent and tone.

> One day, a crow was sitting all on his tod in a tree at the edge of the forest, when up comes this fox. The crow had a bit of cheese in his gate and the fox took a fancy to it, and being a bit of a tea-leaf decided to nick it. So he thinks to himself 'I'll butter him up' – the crow that is. 'Wat'cha'mate, you're looking 'ighly today, you must be the dead 'ighliest bird in the forest'. The crow had been had, but the fox didn't let up. 'Cor blimey, I bet a beautiful bird like you has got a really casual voice to go with it'. The crow, being sort a' big headed, started to warble. Course, when he opened his mouth the cheese fell out. The fox copped the cheese and bundled off into the forest, leaving the crow yelling his head off.

The same stimulus, and yet the response is so different. It may sometimes prove a problem in coping with groups all working at different rates and depths. But the advantages of such personal freedom of expression usually outweighs this. One person may take a fairly literal approach to the material given, another will use far more imagination. One of the original aims of the exercise was to spark off thinking about words and language and the way local expressions give colour.

This third example is from the Welsh border and it is interesting to note how the speaker has used his imagination to develop the story and include a range of local idioms.

> Well, it was top of the day like and there's 'owd crow sat up in a tree and he's got a lump of cheese he's sklend off somewhere, and he's sat with it in his beak, see, just holding it like – you know. Anyhow, along a bit there's an old fox like scrawling down under the hedge. Flenny as a rook he is and his old ears is flat again his head, you see. Well, just now he twigs what he's after, specmate at his lump of cheese, you know. So anyroad up, he's foxed for a bit, can a' see how he's goin' for it. Well, it's twice round the wrekin and out through the needle's eye, like, but he's sharp like and after a bit he reckons on smarming him up see. So, he's down under the brush, like, just like he does it every day; sees this old crow bottoms up, so to say. Well, anyroad, he looks up nice as you like, and says 'How been ye, matey, all right?' Old crow donna twig it see and next half brush's got it nailed. 'Fair wind up there, aint it? Them feathers is

there though, never a whistle in her.' Course, old crow's lapping it up, preening herself fair like a weathercock, and foxey says to him 'you're look right like a weathercock top o' yon church yonda'. The ol' crow he takes it on like the top of the churn. 'I warrant you'll sing better an' him though. Feel like oilin ye neck?' Fox is taking him on, see, 'n the old crow puffs out his old chest and lets out challing. Course, first off opens his mouth and out falls the cheese – just what foxy wants, see, and he's there waiting for it, all mouth he is. One bite he's off up the ride laughin' to himself. Well, you never saw the like and matey's up there calling like he's sat on a scrag o' gorse.

Some improvisations will be over quickly, just using the stimulus and be gone, others will develop and sprawl out, taking byways and nighways. Our opportunities are to see how people meet the responses and help them to develop the best qualities and overcome the weaker elements. Provided our own purposes are clear, we shall be able so use the responses to enrich understanding and pleasure in literature.

(b) Improvisation is rarely the single, solo response – more often it is a chance to work together

It is people encountering people, so that we do not just develop our understanding of literature, but understand how ideas in different ways can be pooled, how they can be sifted, sorted and shared finally to present a group expression which has unity and shape.

More than one child has looked forward to periods of drama as that time when 'you get to know people'. There seems still a surprising amount of time in school when it is not permitted to talk to others or meet people and form relationships. In developing improvisations you have to learn how to work with all temperaments and abilities. You learn to adjust, to circumvent awkwardness and to utilize all kinds of talent. People learn from each other and not just the teacher.

(c) Improvisation takes place NOW!

It enables us to appreciate and discover the heritage of literature in this present moment of time. So, the permanent, the fixed, comes alongside the transient, the immediate. In 1961, Jean Louis Barrault gave, at Oxford, a lecture called 'The Phenomenon of Theatre'. Although he is talking about professional theatre, he is closely relating his discussion to the human and what might in the best sense be called educational. When he was talking about the link between actor and audience, or between actor and actor, he paused for quite some time:

> I now compare the theatre with the other arts; there is apparently not much room for theatre. The other arts satisfy all our senses – painting in a straightforward manner satisfies the sense of vision – music the sense of hearing – poetry satisfies our understanding – and so on until we reach the culinary art which satisfies the papillae of our tongue. I cannot very well see where theatre can take its place – all our very definite senses are reached by the other arts. But they are reached one after the other: when we look at a picture theoretically we are deaf, we only have eyes; when we listen to music we often close our eyes, we only have ears.

Then the pause, after which he continued:

> At this moment I would like you to be well aware of the present instant. For some time I have been talking to you in abstract terms, but at this moment, now, this very second, the present appears to us in a concrete manner, we can grasp it, we can touch it. Sounds and shapes, colours, waves of every kind, strike us from all sides. At each instant of the present, the future is changed to the past, that which waited life shines like lightning and at once becomes the past, the abstract concept of what is to come, in contact with the concrete reality, is transformed into abstract recollection of the past.
>
> So it is uniquely at the lightning moment of the present that life exists, that reality is here, concrete, and it is precisely that moment we have come to grasp.
>
> It is not surprising to come to realize that what men speak of most the FUTURE and the PAST – is what does not exist, and that what does exist – the PRESENT – is actually ungraspable? We need an art capable of recreating life, accurately observed, from the standpoint of the present, and not from the standpoint of colour and shape like painting, or sound like music, but from the standpoint of co-existence of sensations.

Each person who reads this page will respond to it in a given moment in time. Were this a conversation, there would be this co-existence and what was said by each person would be modified by the contribution of the other. This is part of the nature of improvisation.

INTRODUCING THE LITERATURE

Any good teacher knows the value of experience prior to analysis and understanding. And perhaps one of the simplest ways is to introduce the plot or some aspect of the story before we go on to work with or talk about or read or explore it in any other way with our children.

There are hundreds of stories suitable for acting. If the story is taken to suit the age, the range, the outlook of the children, we can almost certainly introduce it in dramatic terms. The narrator is a useful device – he can be used in simple stories or employed in the most complex situations. The teacher himself might tell the narrative while it is being acted out. From even this simple approach, we can gain a physical, three-dimensional preparation, and bring the hitherto passive listeners into more active participation in the situation.

You can see it at work in Peter Weiss' play *Marat/Sade*, where the Herald briefly at the outset describes each character in turn. He is always ready to step into the action to help the flow if things don't go smoothly and he reminds the actors in context of what happens next.

Getting to know the plot or story in this way prepares for the next stage and already begins questions rising in the mind. In David Halliwell's *Little Malcolm* we find Malcolm Scrawdyke and his cronies from the Huddersfield Art College seeking revenge on Mr Allard, their Principal, for having suspended Scrawdyke. Their plan of action is to steal a painting from the Art Gallery, and then later, capture the Principal and blackmail him into breaking the painting, to give them a real strong hold over him. In order to gain some insight into the situation they act it out imaginatively in the security of Scrawdyke's flat and as they proceed they keep asking questions and making discoveries.

It is very similar to what we are doing when we are introducing our story through dramatic play. To help us into the literature, we are beginning to develop ideas and insight into the particular situation. David Halliwell's play focuses other important aspects of work in drama.

Through the play within the play, the characters are acting out their own fantasies and giving expression to their imaginations. They're using drama as sublimation and using imaginative experiences to work out their own personal dislikes and animosities.

It is an interesting play because it brings out the fact that it is possible to use drama both to escape to life or from it. In itself improvisation or drama is neither good nor bad – it is what we do with it that's so important. We can use it to escape from a situation, to avoid a situation, or to get rid of a situation. It's up to us to make sure that we know where we are aiming to go.

So, improvisation can introduce a plot. It can introduce to us a story, so that we have some understanding of its shape and its nature and character. It can also help us to understand it in present day terms. Literature has stood the test of time, but quite often it has been with us for so long that we have either become so accustomed to it we lose sight of its significance, or it is expressed in words and terms and terminology which we find difficult to follow. Before I began working towards a production of Euripides' play, *Women of Troy*, with some students, they had read through the text. Most of them found it remote and lacking in significance. So we sat down for a short while and discussed its theme. What ideas were there behind the play? Then, in groups, the students went away to work on scenes about today. They improvised a series of short plays based on expression of the ideas which they felt to be underlying the play by Euripides.

Each of the improvisations was connected with present day authoritarianism. Local authorities or officials used their power without regard for the individual. In one scene officials took away a young child from its mother because the child, it was claimed, was not getting proper care and protection. In another, first furniture was confiscated to pay for rent arrears, then the child was removed because there was no home. The improvisations radically affected the approach to the Greek text. From that time forward the cast sensed the strength, power and the contemporary significance of the play. It seems especially important when we are studying text for examination purposes, that we should feel confident in employing this method to help make the work both understandable and acceptable and form a counterbalance to the analytical study which usually preoccupies teachers.

Supposing we were studying *Romeo and Juliet* and we were anxious for the play to be seen in present day terms, even before we began considering the text, it would be possible to begin with some improvisations designed to illustrate the problems and

prejudices which cause antagonism between families. Once
initial conflicts had been illustrated by acting them, it would be
possible to clarify the plot at one point by another supposition –
supposing one of the families has a son and the other a daughter,
and they become interested in each other. Answers from one
group faced with this question went like this:

> In each family there's a certain amount of reason, but one assumes
> that perhaps ten or fifteen years have gone past and probably at least
> ten years of not talking.
> This would build up more and more antagonism, because they're
> just not communicating with one another.
> Because of the feeling of most women, I think the mothers are
> going to be especially guarded.
> Well, especially the son's mother.
> The mothers are going to be especially possessive and find some-
> thing wrong.
> There could be the two opposite points: the one side trying
> desperately to make friends and make it up, and the others being
> dogmatic and not having anything to do with them.

Here is part of an improvisation which followed this discussion:

First Family

'Do you know what time he's coming in tonight?'
'What?'
'Do you know what time he's coming in tonight – John? I hope
you don't mind, not too tired or anything, but could you talk to
him?'
'Talk to him?'
'Well, just have a talk to him. You know what it's like, we used
to be able to talk, but now he's gone so independent I can't get
through to him.'
'Well, what's there to talk about, the lad's got his own life to live,
good God!'
'Yes, but he might be meeting up with somebody I don't like.'
'Meeting up with somebody you don't like! You talk in circles.'
'He might be going out with Jackie next door; could you talk to
him?'
'Well, it's a change if it's birds not motorbikes, isn't it?'
'Well, it might be a particular bird, and I don't like that particular
bird's mother.'
'Well, she always seems to be a fairly nice young girl. We haven't
spoken to them for God knows how long, but that's nothing against
her, is it?'

'Would you talk to him about it? Just find out what there is, what he can see in her – in that family.'

'If you insist.'

Second Family

'I will not have it.'

'Please, dear, try and understand. He's quite a nice boy.'

'Have you seen him – long hair, motorbike, leather jacket, the lot!'

'He looks a bit scruffy, but he's very helpful.'

'Up to the ears in muck and oil every day of the week.'

'He's very considerate – I think he's nice to Jackie.'

'Considerate towards you, what's he done for you.'

'Well, he's always helping in little ways.'

'Like what?'

'Well, he always says hello, and . . . '

'Greasing, that's all that is. That's no friend, that's greasing.'

From exploration of this kind can come discovery of aspects of character, attitudes of mind, so that thinking is opened up and we begin to prepare our minds for the text. Shakespeare's *Romeo and Juliet* can be approached then with questions and an interest already aroused. How does the play vary from our scenes? Which attitudes are different from ours? The text will have acquired already certain lifts and awareness. It is possible to go through a play seeing most of its situations in modern terms and expressing the thoughts in today's language.

Now, this practice of paraphrase sometimes leads to objections being raised. One complaint is that 'Shakespeare said it so well – I can't say it any better'. This is to miss the point. Nobody is asking anyone to attempt an improvement of the bard. What is being attempted is a clarification of the thoughts expressed in one's own words. This means that the words have had to be thought through instead of leaving them as a rather vague concept. It is very easy to have a half recollection or belief that you understand what something means. In rehearsals it is interesting when faced with a scene like that in which Friar Laurence and Romeo meet. Phrasing and language are sometimes complex and not easy to communicate. Using one's own words is a good starting point. In any study of the text, whether for production or not, it is useful to work on one scene with different people playing the parts in improvisations. So actors see other people playing the part that they are going to act.

So it was that Julie, who was acting the part of the Nurse in a production of the play, came to play the role of Romeo at one rehearsal. She was trying to keep as close as she could to the text in thought and ideas, but using her own words. Afterwards she realized more about the characters and herself. She remarked: 'You know, that's just how I talk to my mother'. She was arguing with Friar Laurence and saying, 'How can you expect to appreciate me unless you've my heart, unless you're my age, unless you have my feelings'. Such an introduction to many scenes invited a comparison between versions, an approach to literature with questions and a discovery that literature is about people.

It would be possible to begin by considering, through improvisation, any of the characters: the Nurse, or Tybalt, Mercutio, Lady Capulet, or Paris, and use any of them as a starting point. Nor does it have to be Shakespeare; it might be Gawain and the Green Knight; it could be Pip, Miss Havisham, the Convict, Anne Frank. If we work on it in our terms, to start with, we are preparing the ground in a stimulating way.

Improvisation, then, may prepare us to understand plot, theme and character in terms of human beings, people who are reacting, working with, encountering other people – a good foundation for any literary appreciation.

EXPLORING LITERATURE

Having discovered a way in, we find it easier to explore the works more fully. Whenever a play, or a novel or a poem, is being studied analytically, it is easy to do so much dissection that the piece itself becomes lost or obscured. It has become clear that, from a whole series of improvisations based on ideas from earliest primitive story, drama and poetry to the most modern, that if one takes a look first of all at the piece as a unity, seeing it at a distance from the very beginning, then it is easier to appreciate the sections as part of the whole. We do this by reading the play, or novel and then making a breakdown or summary, trying to follow its phases or rhythmic sections. In fact, what we are doing is a literary exercise, though we are doing it for a non-literary purpose. It comes as part of our determination to grasp the whole of the text.

Here we are still using improvisation but in a different form, and with a different aim. We are now trying to come as close as we can to the text, though never aiming to learn it. Even when rehearsing a play for performance, I say: 'Don't learn the text'. I don't mean you haven't to *know* the text, because you do, but don't *try* to learn it. When rehearsing, I was always struck by the fact that I, as the Producer, who had made no attempt to learn the text, always seemed to know the play better than those who were desperately trying to learn it. And, of course, that was the answer – my mind had an openness with desire to understand, but as soon as any attempt is made to learn it the mind clamps up and nothing can pass into it so easily. The aim must be to open up so that ideas can flow through and into the understanding.

The process is one of coming to terms with what the play is about, not worrying about the actual words, though the more these are understood, the closer the improvisation is to it. It is both a very much quicker and a very much surer process because the understanding is from inside.

Here is the opening section of Harold Pinter's *A Slight Ache*, followed by an improvisation based on the same section.

FLORA: Have you noticed the honeysuckle this morning?
EDWARD: The what?
FLORA: The honeysuckle.
EDWARD: Honeysuckle? Where?
FLORA: By the back gate, Edward.
EDWARD: Is that honeysuckle? I thought it was ... convolvulus, or something.
FLORA: But you know it's honeysuckle.
EDWARD: I tell you I thought it was convolvulus.
(*Pause.*)
FLORA: It's in wonderful flower.
EDWARD: I must look.
FLORA: The whole garden's in flower this morning. The clematis. The convolvulus. Everything. I was out at seven. I stood by the pool.
EDWARD: Did you say – that the convolvulus was in flower?
FLORA: Yes.
EDWARD: But good God, you just denied there was any.
FLORA: I was talking about the honeysuckle.
EDWARD: About the what?
FLORA (*calmly*): Edward – you know that shrub outside the toolshed.
EDWARD: Yes, yes.
FLORA: That's convolvulus.
EDWARD: That?

FLORA: Yes.
EDWARD: Oh.
(*Pause.*)
I thought it was japonica.
FLORA: Oh, good Lord no.
EDWARD: Pass the teapot, please.
(*Pause. She pours tea for him.*)
I don't see why I should be expected to distinguish between these plants. It's not my job.
FLORA: You know perfectly well what grows in your garden.
EDWARD: Quite the contrary. It is clear that I don't.
(*Pause.*)
FLORA (*rising*): I was up at seven. I stood by the pool. The peace. And everything in flower. The sun was up. You should work in the garden this morning. We could put up the canopy.
EDWARD: The canopy? What for?
FLORA: To shade you from the sun.
EDWARD: Is there a breeze?
FLORA: A light one.
EDWARD: It's very treacherous weather, you know.
(*Pause.*)
FLORA: Do you know what today is?
EDWARD: Saturday.
FLORA: It's the longest day of the year.
EDWARD: Really?
FLORA: It's the height of summer today.
EDWARD: Cover the marmalade.
FLORA: What?
EDWARD: Cover the pot. There's a wasp. (*He puts the paper down on the table.*) Don't move. Keep still. What are you doing?
FLORA: Covering the pot.
EDWARD: Don't move. Leave it. Keep still.
(*Pause.*)
Give me the 'Telegraph'.
FLORA: Don't hit it. It'll bite.
EDWARD: Bite? What do you mean, bite? Keep still.
(*Pause.*)
It's landing.
FLORA: It's going in the pot.
EDWARD: Give me the lid.
FLORA: It's in.
EDWARD: Give me the lid.
FLORA: I'll do it.
EDWARD: Give it to me! Now ... Slowly ...
FLORA: What are you doing?

EDWARD: Be quiet. Slowly ... carefully ... on ... the ... pot!
Ha-ha-ha. Very good.
(*He sits on a chair to the right of the table.*)
FLORA: Now he's in the marmalade.
EDWARD: Precisely.
(*Pause. She sits on a chair to the left of the table and reads the 'Telegraph'.*)
FLORA: Can you hear him?
EDWARD: Hear him?
FLORA: Buzzing.
EDWARD: Nonsense. How can you hear him? It's an earthenware lid.
FLORA: He's becoming frantic.
EDWARD: Rubbish. Take it away from the table.
FLORA: What shall I do with it?
EDWARD: Put it in the sink and drown it.
FLORA: It'll fly out and bite me.
EDWARD: It will not bite you! Wasps don't bite. Anyway, it won't
fly out. It's stuck. It'll drown where it is, in the marmalade.
FLORA: What a horrible death.
EDWARD: On the contrary.
(*Pause.*)
FLORA: Have you got something in your eyes?
EDWARD: No. Why do you ask?
FLORA: You keep clenching them, blinking them.
EDWARD: I have a slight ache in them.
FLORA: Oh, dear.
EDWARD: Yes, a slight ache. As if I hadn't slept.
FLORA: Did you sleep, Edward?
EDWARD: Of course I slept. Uninterrupted. As always.
FLORA: And yet you feel tired.
EDWARD: I didn't say I felt tired. I merely said I had a slight ache in
my eyes.
FLORA: Why is that, then?
EDWARD: I really don't know.
(*Pause.*)
FLORA: Oh goodness!
EDWARD: What is it?
FLORA: I can see it. It's trying to come out.
EDWARD: How can it?
FLORA: Through the hole. It's trying to crawl out, through the
spoon-hole.
EDWARD: Mmmnn, yes. Can't do it, of course. (*Silent pause.*)
Well, let's kill it, for goodness' sake.
FLORA: Yes, let's, But how?
EDWARD: Bring it out on the spoon and squash it on a plate.

FLORA: It'll fly away. It'll bite.
EDWARD: If you don't stop saying that word I shall leave this table.
FLORA: But wasps do bite.
EDWARD: They don't bite. They sting. It's snakes . . . that bite.
FLORA: What about horseflies?
(*Pause.*)
EDWARD (*to himself*): Horseflies suck.
(*Pause.*)
FLORA (*tentatively*): If we . . . if we wait long enough, I suppose it'll choke to death. It'll suffocate in the marmalade.
EDWARD (*briskly*): You do know I've got work to do this morning, don't you? I can't spend the whole day worrying about a wasp.
FLORA: Well, kill it.
EDWARD: You want to kill it?
FLORA: Yes.
EDWARD: Very well. Pass me the hot water jug.
FLORA: What are you going to do?
EDWARD: Scald it. Give it to me.

The actors looked at the play and decided that, in order to improvise this, they had to take ideas and notice how they were shaped in relation to the pauses. They noticed the pauses were powerful. They explained: 'After a thought – thoughts have been going on – then there's usually a pause, a dramatic pause, and then there is another thought sequence.' 'We took the first couple of pages and looked at the thought sequence and tried to remember them, and then worked on them, but always thinking about what Pinter wants – you in relation to what Pinter wants.'

'Did you see the honeysuckle this morning?'
'The what?'
'The honeysuckle.'
'Honeysuckle? Where?'
'In the garden. By the back gate.'
'Is that honeysuckle? I thought it was Convolvulus.'
'You know it's honeysuckle; I was up this morning, went in the garden . . . beautiful, you know . . . lovely morning . . . went down by the pool. . . . '
'Isn't it convolvulus?'
'No, honeysuckle – you know your own garden, Edward.'
'It seems I don't! I thought we had some convolvulus.'
'Do you know what day it is?'
'Saturday.'
'Longest day of the year.'

'Really?'

'Height of summer.'

'Cover the pot.'

'What?'

'Cover the pot.'

'Cover the what?'

'There's a wasp – don't move – what are you doing?'

'Covering the pot.'

'I said don't move. It's going in the marmalade. Cover it up quick. Quick. Give me the lid.'

'It's in.'

'Give me the lid! Slowly. Ha-a-ha.'

'It's in the marmalade.'

'Precisely.'

'What a terrible death.'

'Quite nice in the marmalade really.'

'Oh, can you hear it?'

'Hear what.'

'Hear the wasp, buzzing.'

'Course you can't hear it . . . it's an earthenware lid.'

'What a sticky end.'

'Take it away from the table.'

'But it might jump out and bite me.'

'Wasps don't bite.'

'It might fly out and bite me.'

'Wasps don't BITE – take it away from the table.'

'Ooh, he's trying to get out of the spoon-hole.'

'Can't get out, of course.'

'It can fly out and bite me.'

'Wasps don't BITE. If you say bite again, I shall leave this table.'

'Well, horse-flies bite.'

'Horse-flies suck.'

'Oh.'

'Do you want me to kill it?'

'Yes.'

'Pass the hot water jug.'

'What for?'

'I'm going to scald it. Give it to me.

The method they summed up like this: 'We read through the play – split it up and made a list of thoughts the day before. Then we talked it over. Altogether it took about half an hour, at the most.'

People will often say that improvising takes a long time. It is, in fact, a short cut. Once an American lady came over when I was rehearsing a play. She said: 'Yes, it's all very well, this improvisation, but could you work this way if you only had eight weeks?'

And I said: 'But I've only got six!' It is true, it looks, it seems a very long process, until you begin. Once you approach the text, the literature, in this way, with a particular end in view, it is in fact a much quicker process and you find that it's a technique which builds up.

This works with any kind of play. People will sometimes say: 'It's all very well when there is a plot you can work on, but what happens when it's another kind of play?' You have to make discoveries about it. I once gave Ann Jellicoe's 'Sport of my Mad Mother' to a group to work on in this way. They found it very difficult. They came to me and said, 'We can't improvise this!' I asked, 'Why not?' and we discussed the play. They went away and came back three times like this and said, 'It's impossible and anyway not worth it', but on the fourth time they came back and said, 'Hey, this is marvellous'. It was only because working on it in a three-dimensional way, instead of only reading it as something on the page, that they were able to discover the text.

It is surprising that so many teachers still need to be reminded that when studying a dramatic text we need to see it in terms of acting. It seems to me that, with most writing, acting can help us discover the literature. As soon as we see it in terms of people, responding to people, in terms of the present situation, we begin to get far more from it. In this kind of improvisation we are both synthesizing and examining the structure. The reading has a practical expression and it still seems a sound educational principle that to retain ideas you need to *do* something with them. Or it may be useful to move outside the text to raise questions and clarify some aspects. For instance, improvisations can help lead into a scene or illustrate repeated dialogue or action.

Or our exploratory acting can try to create an atmosphere, mood, or situation, designed to give a greater sense of the literature being worked upon. Sometimes clarification may come in the nature of a happening. Once when I was working on *Othello* and discussing with the girl who was playing Desdemona her feelings when Othello attacked her verbally, she said she felt very much that she would have fought back and have given Othello a piece of her mind. She couldn't understand how Desdemona could remain so shattered by this. We built up an improvisation and during this I said: 'It's almost as if he's hit you physically'. Her reply was that in such a situation she would hit back. So we built up our improvisation, in the middle of which I slapped her face. For a few moments she was stunned and then suddenly a smile came across her face and she said: 'I see what you mean'. And out of this happening she derived insight and understanding of the situation.

It is the things which happen in our lives which make the greatest impression on us. Talk is less effective when it is unsupported by action. Once asked to give a talk about Modern Theatre, I was especially requested to make some reference to Happenings. I didn't think it sensible only to *talk* about Happenings, so I arranged that one should take place in the middle of the section about them. The audience was shocked at the intrusion and it was that small section of the evening which occupied almost all of the discussion. All the other things I had *said* that evening were ignored. People remembered what had *happened*.

It is possible to employ improvisation in all kinds of ways and towards other literary discoveries. Often when looking at verse pattern in dramatic verse, we have explored the rhythm by actually dancing it out. Lines of Shakespeare have often found additional significance through physical realization. We use the expression 'poetic feet' for a good reason – as soon as the rhythm is felt in the feet and the body, and danced in relation to another character, further understanding develops.

When a young actor was working on his part in *Richard III*, he had this line to say: 'Woe, woe, for England not a whit for me'. In rehearsal he said it rather inexpressively, until he danced and moved it with his whole body and he realized: 'Hey, it's like a bell tolling, isn't it – it's "W-o-e, w-o-e, for England, not a whit for me" '. By feeling this physical presence of the lines in himself, he had discovered how to communicate the meaning. In a movement pattern he had come closer to aspects of dramatic appreciation and to fulfilment of the text and, of course, a richer literary approach.

DEVELOPING DRAMA

The more we appreciate, experience and understand how the playwright, how the novelist, how the poet works, in language and in all these other ways, the more there is to feed back into the work which we ourselves are doing, especially the drama we ourselves are creating.

Although Caldwell Cook's book *The Play Way* was written at the beginning of this century, much of its idea and method is still very modern in outlook. His expression and turn of phrase may seem dated, but the approach is the same as that applauded and recommended today. He doesn't actually use the word improvisation, but it is just that which he is employing as the means to help youngsters to discover literature:

> Now as touching originality, it is I think a mistake to encourage children to invent stories and characters for themselves. They will be all too apt to set the scene in the cellar of a London Bank, or in the Wild West Canyon, or in the Boarding House of a Public School, and to choose for their protagonist a detective, or a bush ranger, or one of those caricatures of boyhood who strut and fret their hours in magazines written for schoolboys, and then are heard no more. This side of their interest must not be neglected in school work, but we have always found a place for that crude expression of their youthful tastes in preliminary exercises – the asides from the main business.

There are no restrictions at first, the main purpose was that the children should exercise themselves in oral composition. Early practice was not hampered by an exacting literary taste and he goes on to suggest how he just accepts, the brash, the momentary, the charade type 'play-it-out' approach in this early work.

> It remains, then, for them either to invent a new, brand new, romantic story, or to borrow one, but the experiment in inventing your plot is so difficult and attended with so many risks of disaster that it is wiser to follow the example of Chaucer, Spencer, Shakespeare, Milton and all the other great poets, and found your story upon the firm traditional story.

You don't have to take it exactly as you find it, the story is there and you can use it if you've got the skill, as some of these people did. But by employing the plot you have the freedom and yet the security of an outline. Having established a story, you can then develop ideas.

> Persons and events exist already; characterization and plot, those twin deities of drama, have been wed together in the tale for perhaps

five hundred years, perhaps two thousand years, and in making their play with what additions and modifications are over, the children are making but one more version of a tale that has outlived, or rather lived through a thousand versions.

The approach may be extended in many ways. We recently took aspects of Abraham Lincoln's life as our literature and developed a play around it. The material was in no way restricting and the end product reflected the attitudes and outlook of our own day and age. Techniques and approach to it reflect our present contempt for authority. Later, the musical *Hair* opened in London, with some strikingly similar approaches and using very similar material. There was in one song a 'Happy Birthday, Aby Baby' and in the other pop song 'Four Score and Seven Years Abo' the opening of the Gettysburg Speech, set to music. The young people I was working with took this Gettysburg Speech and gave, in satirical improvisation, their version of how they thought it might have come to be written.

SECRETARY: Ah, good morning, and what can I do for you today, Sir?

LINCOLN: Ah, um, yes. I've got a letter for some bod up in Pennysylvania wanting us to open a graveyard for them. And I've nothing doing on the 19th. How about one of those nice little speeches of yours?

SECRETARY: But what would you like? I could do you a long tearjerker about the gallant lads in blue . . .

LINCOLN: Oh no, no, no. Those bloody senators are milking that for all they are worth; anyway, I'm sick and tired of the army. All those bruised coloured sods following each other around. No! We'd better have it a bit shorter than usual and stirring and make them think for a change.

SECRETARY: Yes, but we must be very careful not to lose this country boy image we've worked very hard to build. We mustn't lose that. I tell you what, appeal to their sense of history, something about the revolution. They always . . .

LINCOLN: No, no, no. It's been done over and over.

SECRETARY: Ah, but not like this, you see. If we mix some of your equality ideas that we use in your election speeches . . .

LINCOLN: Oh.

SECRETARY: And shove in a bit of down-home religion for the old folks and a few long words for the historians to think about in a few hundred years . . .

LINCOLN: Yes, I like that. Lincoln, they'll say, man or myth? . . . Was he the greatest man since Christ?

SECRETARY: Yes. Now when *was* the revolution – was it 1776 or 77?

LINCOLN: '77, I think.

SECRETARY: That's right, it's '76, '76, 'cos I've got a memorial tankard with the date on it, so it's 87 years ago. You could say . . .

LINCOLN: Eighty seven years ago.

SECRETARY: No, we'll go all Shakespearean and say 'Four Score and Seven years ago.'

LINCOLN: Four score and seven . . .

SECRETARY: Our fathers brought forth to this continent a new nation.

LINCOLN: A new nation . . .

SECRETARY: Conceived in liberty.

LINCOLN: Conceived in liberty . . .

SECRETARY: Dedicated to the proposition that all men are created equal.

LINCOLN: All men are created equal . . . Oh no, nobody believes that stuff nowadays.

SECRETARY: It was you that created them equal in the first place.

LINCOLN: Was it? I wish you'd tell me what you're putting in my speeches. You know I don't always read them before I perform in public. Go on, then – it's nice so far.

SECRETARY: You could say 'We are fighting – no – we are engaged'.

LINCOLN: Why?

SECRETARY: 'We are engaged with great Civil War testing and trying.'

LINCOLN: Trying . . .

SECRETARY: 'Testing whether this nation or any other so dedicated . . . '

LINCOLN: Dedicated . . .

SECRETARY: How's that so far?

LINCOLN: That's beautiful. These long words are tremendous: conceived in liberty – dedicated to the proposition. You're marvellous.

SECRETARY: O.K. Then we could say something like 'We are met on a battle-field to dedicate a piece of that field as a . . . '

LINCOLN: Haven of rest.

SECRETARY: Graveyard, keep it simple.

LINCOLN: Haven of rest.

SECRETARY: As a final haven of rest for those men who gave their lives that this nation might live.

LINCOLN: Gettysburg, that's the battle-field place, isn't it? The War's getting me down. What was it you said: 'Gave their lives that this nation might live. Gave their lives 'cos I bloody told them to. How many copped it at this Gettysburg anyway?

SECRETARY: About forty-six thousand and thirty-seven of those were Generals.

LINCOLN: Buried in the same grave as the soldiers – there's your equality. All men are created equal. It's me that does it – they couldn't be equal without me.

SECRETARY: Well, then I thought we could go deeper, by saying: 'We cannot consecrate this ground because those men who died here have already hallowed it with their blood.'

LINCOLN: Hallowed with their blood – you are a poet!

SECRETARY: And then you could end up something like: 'That those dead shall not have died in vain – that this nation, under God, shall have a new birth of freedom and that the Government of the people, by the people, for the people, shall not perish from the earth'.

LINCOLN: That's it. Keep their noses to the grindstone. More money for the White House piggy-bank and they'll think they are doing it for democracy. We've got a winner there. Well, look, you write it out and let me have it in time for tonight. I feel more like a drink. I've got to meet old Todd bod's parents for dinner tonight and I could use a couple of quickies first.

Here is illustrated the irreverence which we are now prepared to give to classic moments like this, the questioning which it raises and above all the way in which the improvisers see that speech in the light of present day electioneering speeches – the political image and the new sham of the speech written *for* the politician. Out of this and other improvisations was developed a whole musical, the *Abraham Lincoln Show*, presented with contrasting, and often confusing, ideas in an attempt to make accepted literary moments questioned and re-questioned in the minds of the audience.

Or, illustrating literary perception and interpretation at a different level, we might take a ballad of Eleanor Rigby by the Beatles. This poem in a pop song played to some young people brought this kind of response:

Well, we started off just looking at the theme of the poem, considering nothing else, just the theme of loneliness, and we went away from the theme a bit by taking the sort of loneliness which is the most awful kind – being lonely in a crowd. We thought of an improvisation in which three of us were having a very strong discussion at a party, and somebody else coming in and wanting to try and get in on the discussion, the talking, wanting to present herself as the life and soul of the party. She was just getting cold stares all the time. And she kept going out and coming back and trying to induce people to some drinks which she had brought, and she'd start giggling and laughing, until finally we would just give her the cold shoulder and eventually she would go.

That was one level of loneliness, but we also looked at others. We saw the other three chatting away happily socializing. They were, in fact, lonely as well, because not one of them was listening to the other; they were talking away and being very lonely. And we saw Father Mackenzie . . .

He isn't a lonely figure in the same way as the other three, though; his loneliness is self imposed to some extent. Eleanor Rigby is a lonely figure because of what is inside herself, I suppose, and her attitude to the world, which makes the world's attitude to her, but Father Mackenzie's loneliness comes from within himself – voluntarily then, to some extent.

I think that after we got to this point we then started to look at what was actually in the poem again, coming back to the poem, and seeing what incidents occurred within the poem to relate the imagery, the rice which he picks up after the wedding, a symbol of perhaps togetherness and happiness. We thought that perhaps the party that would be given as a form of celebration, like the wedding cake, shall we say, or christening cake, or something like this, which you could take away and not eat but keep in a box.

One of the things that comes out is where are all those people – where have they come from? Perhaps when she does go out for the drinks, or take a coat, there are people saying 'Who is she?' 'Where does she come from?'

How much literary appreciation rises from the attempt at developing this drama!

Let me give Jean Louis Barrault the last words which emphasize this element of our opportunity and underline some of the qualities which as soon as you start acting you find you are working with:

If the actor is to be able to represent, in a selected and crystallized form, a human prototype, he will have had to draw on a great deal of love. It is only through the greatest love that one can fit perfectly inside another's skin. You well know that lovers come to have the same colour eyes, the same way of looking, the same tone of voice, the same handwriting. Sincere lovers come to be infected by simulation – the phenomenon of mimetism. By force of love, and love not only of men but of life, one lends to life a human soul. Of course, if I lend you all my love, I will lend you my heart and my soul, and just as I believe you have both my heart and my soul, so I believe everything in life will assume a human form, everything will have a soul. The phenomenon of lending a soul to everything that surrounds us is called animism, the oak then becomes the king of the forest, the lion the king of the animals, the wind is a mischievous lad, fire a wicked person, liberty is a woman. And it is through these two phenomena which result from the greatest love, mimetism and animism, that we come to be able to fit perfectly inside the skin of others and to change personality. It seems to me that in this way the theatrical phenomenon takes place as far as the actor goes. Here we are opposed to exhibitionism and narcissism. I have in this breakdown of the theatre overtaken the first two objections, social delusion and individual impotence, and I have replaced them by public usefulness and the greatest love of man.

And I think that if we see improvisation and literature come together, we should recognize that what we are going for is a greater insight into ourselves and a deeper and fuller concern for other people.

3. Drama and Education: Subject or System?

Dorothy Heathcote

MUCH ATTENTION has been given to Drama as a subject, but in comparison very little to Drama as a system. I therefore shall consider the latter. Drama in education can be sub-divided *ad infinitum* depending upon how many persons happen to be discussing it at any one moment and what interests they profess to. The terms are only too familiar – the precise meanings too vague. I refer to divisions such as improvisation, role-playing, dance-drama, socio-drama and so on. These are all conventional sub-divisions of a larger field. It is more relevant to my purpose deliberately to keep the field large and whole and sectionalize my cultivator – the teacher. What do all teachers hold in common? We can assume the wish to communicate, or at least the responsibility for communication (if only of the one-way type) to be accepted. One can also assume interest in subject area, presumably, too, a modicum of concern with measurement of that which has been communicated, together with some basic training *for* the job and the need to survive *in* the job. No one teaches a teacher how to teach. Teachers are made in the classroom during confrontations with their classes, and the product they become is a result of their need to survive and the ways they devise to do this. In my view insufficient emphasis is placed upon this during the training period or at any time later when new skills are required.

One should be prepared to define one's terms. For the present purpose I will define a teacher as 'one who creates learning situations for others'. That is, his energies and skills are at the service, during the professional situation, of his pupils. A teacher's rewards come because those energies flow into other people and therefore can make the return journey through the teacher's own intake ability from his classes. The *total* person a teacher is, is employed in this task, properly filtered through the professional principles and duties. What he *knows* he requires to communicate. What he *is* is his means of achieving this.

I define educational drama as being 'anything which involves persons in active role-taking situations in which attitudes, not characters, are the chief concern, lived at life-rate (i.e. discovery *at this moment*, not memory based) and obeying the natural laws of the medium'. I regard these as being (i) a willing suspension of disbelief (ii) agreement to pretence (iii) employing all past experiences available to the group at the present moment and any conjecture of imagination they are capable of, in an attempt to create a living, moving picture of life, which aims at surprise and discovery for the participants rather than for any onlookers. The scope of this is to be defined by story-line and theme, so that the problem with which they grapple is clearly defined. I maintain that problem-solving is the basis of learning and maturation.

Problem-solving[1] in a man extends the work again of learning, It is the capacity to act as if an act were carried out before in fact it is undertaken. It uses past experience, product of prior learning, to predict what may happen if and when certain acts are carried out in conditions given: it (i) multiplies interlocking learnings, (ii) seeks their conscious integration, (iii) provides a ground for more sustaining action, and (iv) sharpens need for evaluations which work out to be productive in their fitting to creation, as acts, in fact, are taken. By means of conscious problem-solving, conscious men increase the range and depth of their conscious knowing of creation's shaping.

Looking at man to note his social nature, we can see that communication is the crucial function. Communication allows men (i) to be inclusive of one another as members of the species, (ii) to integrate their meaning for each other, (iii) to order their transactions to be increasingly supportive, and (iv) to share more fully in communion with their natures. Communication between two human creatures is an act of interlocking their emergent knowings in the sequence of upcoming moments as they share them. As one speaks, the other listens, receiving what is coming for its meaning in the forming of what he then speaks, while the other listens, thus to form a back-and-forth of intercourse which

[1] *Explorations in Creativity*, eds. Ross Mooney and Taher Razik. Harper & Row.

is no less birth-giving in its basic structure than nature offers, elsewhere, for forming fresh conceptions. Communication, done in tune, is a way to know, profoundly, creation's wondrous, ordered working. In the classroom setting, we have as elemental the communicative system between a teacher and a student. We know its basic nature: two creative systems intercoursing, feeding one another.

The teacher is a sender and a receiver; the student is a sender and a receiver. What the teacher sends, the student needs to be able to receive; what the student sends, the teacher needs to be able to receive. As the teacher receives a particular sending from the student, the teacher needs to be able to organize a response which is relevant to what the student can next receive and use; the student, receiving, then organizing his response to be relevant to what the teacher can next receive and use, thus continues the sequence of communication. As each receives and sends, he has to be able to project into the inner world of the other and to sense what is forming there. Then his communication can be meaningful (a means) to the sequential and emergent development of the communication. Otherwise, communication fails; education fails. Communication is the centre of the educative system.

I am concerned then with two main aspects of teaching: the first is the way a teacher confronts his class and the way the two-way flow of communication takes place. This is the living vibrating matter of teaching, firmly based upon mutual respect by each for the other's contribution. A factor which may have to be taken into consideration when training teachers to use drama in education is the varying ways of thinking which are presently being researched into by Liam Hudson[1] and others. I refer to the convergent/divergent types.

(a) *Convergent Thinking*:[2] this is the ability to give the appropriate response, to acquire habits of thought and action which are most acceptable within a culture or subculture – for example, lower-class as compared with middle-class value systems (McGuire and White, 1957). Measures of performances on tests of intelligence, abstract reasoning, space relations, and the ability to listen combine to yield this 'factor in persons.'

(b) *Divergent Thinking*: some, more than others, acquire a capacity

[1] Liam Hudson, *Contrary Imaginations*. Pelican Books.
[2] *Explorations in Creativity*, eds. Ross Mooney and Tahar Razik. Harper & Row.

to devise new forms, come up with fresh ideas, and see deeper meanings in objects, events, inter-personal relationships, and symbolic materials. Measures, such as identifying unforeseen consequences, seeing unusual uses of problems, and sensing new meanings in common situations, now are used to identify the creative person. Although some teachers and parents value creative children and adolescents, many are uncomfortable with them and prefer a degree of conformity (Getzels & Jackson, 1960).

We cannot afford to ignore this in training schemes for quite obvious reasons. The second point concerns the areas of security the teacher gradually acquires and depends upon in his job: teachers require to understand their own security and practice in order that they may gradually push back these security needs and accept more tenuous positions in order that eventually they may teach from positions of calculated risk. I believe very few teachers discover their true teaching thresholds because of timetables and syllabi which disallow the discovery of natural teaching pace and rate. This applies equally to the classes taught. Many may never come to terms with their learning rate until after their school life is over. These security thresholds seem to be (a) *The noise level*. That is the quality in the sound which first causes the teacher's 'panic stations' behaviour to come into operation. I refer to discomfort regarding the noise which the teacher cannot ignore. This is sometimes rooted in guilt, for so much so-called discipline is related to noise level, when in fact noise *quality* is much more relevant. (b) *The space level*. This refers not to emptiness but to the distance the teacher requires to set between himself and the class: (c) *The group-comfort level*, that is, sizes of groups most comfortably and efficiently dealt with in the teacher's subjective view. (d) *The way decisions are achieved* in the classroom. (e) *The 'subject' interests* of the teacher. (f) *The resources* the teacher employs in evaluating the work undertaken. (g) *The variety of registers* available to the teacher in approaching the class.

The noise threshold. If we are going to teach at all well in any circumstances (and I am not here referring only to drama) we must understand the kind and the quality of noise we can take and the point at which we *cannot* take it. Questions like, 'Are you comfortable in class when children discuss and leave you out of it? What if children argue back, or shout at each other across you, or are shifting furniture?' are relevant here. Some teachers are very uncomfortable under one or other of these circumstances, and would be wiser and more efficient never to become involved in such situations. These are not fanciful ideas. It is time to do job-study in teaching, and each individual has to make a start. It is essential that we learn to teach with a modicum of security so that we are not consequently appalled by meeting our thresholds all the time. Some are uncomfortable with even an *appearance* of disorganization. Headmasters looking through windows may have a very powerful effect upon that particular threshold!

The space threshold. I make my contacts most comfortably when classes are close together and near to me. Others require to teach at a distance. This does not make either of us better or worse teachers. Value judgements are irrelevant here; the main consideration is that the teacher personally understands *why* he teaches at the distance he elects to use and the consequent effects of this choice. For many years I wondered at my stupidity in creating such crowded situations which can be uncomfortable and sometimes nauseous, until I understood this requirement and now can accept and employ it positively. I have to create situations in which classes can first throw their behaviour in my face in order that I may make an assessment of needs and therefore of starting points. Also, for drama, I require that a class shall be made to feel like a group. Desks isolate individuals, therefore my instinct is to discard them *unless* I require individual *differences* to emerge, then I hurry to desks in order that *that* behaviour may emerge. Eye impact and eye feedback is important. The teacher who requires the class to look (and feel to be) a small number in a large space, functions very differently from the one who prefers a class to seem a large group in a relatively small space. In fact both these are valuable experiences at relevant times. Once this is consciously understood, changes may be made to employ both when they best serve the needs of the class, the material, and lastly of the teacher who may be more ready to risk-take because of this conscious knowing. Teachers often request empty space for drama, but all areas are space, only some are interrupted upwards by pillars, cupboards and other compendia, some symmetrically by, for example, desks, others circularly by floor patterns, or lighting arrangements. Some focus toward one end. The teacher and class will have a subjective response to all these factors which can be most profitably employed if it is consciously realized in drama work so that strengths and weaknesses of form, for the purpose in hand, may be exploited or circumvented.

The Size of Group Threshold. While relationships are still tenuous I require my classes to function as one group. For some people this is the least happy or convenient grouping. I require the large group for my personal comfort as I need to make personal contact of eye, voice, and group positioning with the class and also I require an immediate feedback of response (good or bad) from them in order to test the relationship and feel the temper of the class. Even when I first began teaching I used this large grouping. The important question is, 'What sizes of group give you security?' Often in training or when teachers first attempt drama the situation becomes closed just at the time when it should remain open. For example advice is often given like 'Begin with small groups or even individuals or pairs', the assumption being that these latter are easier to deal with. In fact, to be realistic, size of group is entirely dependent upon the subjective view of the teacher. The medium is so flexible that it can begin anywhere and function under all circumstances. Every other rule is irrelevant at this point. Once some security is gained, teaching experimentation and other consequent dramatic forms may be explored by the teacher and class when the size of groups employed can be directly related to the aim and purpose of the work done. A whole class working upon a market situation will bring, receive and face totally different experiences than when working in pairs. It should be possible to help a teacher understand the differing consequences of saying, 'Find a partner and work out this,' 'Divide into groups,' 'Everybody is going to be the same character,' 'Go away and lay out your market stalls,' 'Find your houses,' 'Listen to this story then act it,' 'Start with these words, "Don't go in there".' It should also be possible to help a teacher understand the difference between progression which aims at burnishing the drama and that which undertakes to burnish the children. Both are sensible educational aims but there is no doubt in my mind which has priority, though sometimes the play may *appear* to be more important.

A further testing aspect of grouping emerges during periods of discussion. Some teachers require to communicate via them, otherwise they feel a loss of grip when the children turn aside and speak to each other with consequent loss of audibility to the teacher. Trying to ensure that every word spoken is heard by everyone else, except under specific circumstances, leads to loss of efficiency and boredom. Personally I am most secure when the class are ignoring my presence, discussing among themselves, thus enabling me to tune in to the temperature and attitudes of their work and the messages I can receive through ear and eye. Thus I am informed of their *next* need. I can quickly get the gist of the discussion simply by asking. I gain much of my information about groups via identification and empathy and rely less upon verbal interchange. The main thing is that we require to know which we rely upon so that we structure to get what we require, first for our security, later in order to risk-take.

Decision-making and leadership thresholds. Some basic questions here seem to be, 'How do you structure for leadership? Do you appoint your trustworthy and reliable ones proven by time? On which occasions do you require to retain leadership yourself? At what stage, and why, will you challenge weaker personnel to lead? When *don't* you mind who emerges?' Obviously all these situations are of value for different purposes, they are not to be set against each other. The secure teacher can employ them all efficiently and skilfully and inbuild the security of a satisfying result for the class. All this is related to the types and degrees of selection a teacher can allow a class and still retain a feeling of security, and also to the way decisions are taken. I require my classes to decide upon material to be used in order that I may discover what types of themes interest them and at what level they require to work and how they become involved. I also believe that decision-taking is an important educational experience and one means of ensuring involvement. Group decision-taking is not easy but there is nothing quite so revealing of either the needs or resources of any community as making this demand. Drama-making involves groups in a vast range of decision taking, and progression in this field is related to more and more subtlety of feeling, perception, language, social adjustment and drama expertise. I want my classes to learn to make decisions, and to understand the problems and rewards of these decisions, so I regard it as my prime task to ensure that they clearly understand the choice between possibilities, the nature of the decision taken and the demands likely to be put upon them because of the decision taken. This is another reason why drama is such a wonderful educational tool.

The subject interest of the teacher clearly will be biased by the intellectual and emotional capacities of the personality, the quality of training received, and their particular approach. It is obvious that the teacher's own interests in the field may be entirely irrelevant to those of the class. In drama it is especially important that teachers have no rigid rules of (i) how to begin, (ii) which material is suitable, (iii) at what level it will be employed, and (iv) which dramatic forms are most acceptable and rewarding at any age. If teachers begin by using rigid rules their consequent development is often towards closed rather than opening and advancing methods of work becoming available to teacher and class alike as they learn to use themselves, their ideas, and gain the capacity to understand and grapple with the medium.

Evaluation and standards thresholds. This relates to the ways teachers observe and the things they value and therefore look for as they observe. Some retire or withdraw in order to see their classes at work, others intrude. Some identify, others enquire. A class involved in drama will throw up so much behaviour and teaching opportunity that it is impossible to observe everything or to seize upon everything. So it is essential that the teacher learns to be highly sensitive in observing the relevance of what is thrown up and to perceive the classes' needs via their behaviour. This penetration of the surface facts in order to reach the relevant data is highly important because through drama work the teacher stimulates and feeds the hidden or disguised elements in classes' or individuals' behaviour.

Another important area of observation is that of clearly seeing (that is without bias, and minus the blinkers of the teacher's previously devised intent) the present group, its mood and possibilities at any given moment. A clear example of this was seen when an E.S.N. boy rummaging through a dressing-up box to choose clothes suitable for a slave-driver in King Herod's entourage, selected a hangman's black mask and cap. If the teacher's response had been 'wrong period, must intervene', how much would have been buried which was just on the point of emerging *because* in choosing, the boy was crystallizing his ideas and feelings. The teacher waited, saw the boy work in the clothes in the drama and observed the enlarged attitudes bringing to the boy a sureness of approach and from the slaves a clear response to the visual threat he fed to them. At some stage the anachronism may be pointed out and a compromise made but the child's need should dictate the timing of this. This boy eventually said in response to an *interest* being shown in his choice of clothing, 'I'm not bringing these women much life, am I?' And thus some of the reasoning behind his choice became clearer to boy, class and teacher. He had taken a reading of the situation of which he was capable *at that moment* and this is at once both the very stuff and opportunity offered by drama in education: to permit *present* readings to be exposed and explored and through that widened into more subtle and generously-based readings. At first attempts readings (or soundings if preferred) especially of unfamiliar situations are bound to be shallow, socially ramshackle, linguistically hesitant or unsound, artistically tenuous. Time and experience bring a tempering and a tightening of all these. We all take our first readings via our prejudice – a mother's reading of 'mother-type' will employ her direct experiences of being a mother, her own childhood memories, the experiences of others in the group, and in time this range of experiences will become available to challenge, deepen and temper her original reading. So in the action of the drama these experiences become exposed for consideration – either of audiences if *that* is the final purpose of the work, or of the group only, if *that* is the purpose. The teacher requires to be *un*prejudiced and receptive to a vast range of readings, helping the situation by receiving, challenging, helping to develop ideas and above all creating and preserving in the class attitudes of receptivity, non-value judgements and artistic integrity. Surely it should be possible for us to devise situations whereby teachers may learn how to do this *filtered through their own personalities*. Because of my personality, much of the drama my classes work upon is sociologically based as I see a class of children trying to work together *as* a social group, so I give a strong lead in this area with a correspondingly weak one in others.

Teaching Registers. All teachers develop a range of these as part of their survival kit. The difficulty is to be aware of the uses made of them and their real value to the teacher. Drama reflects registers of approach to and confrontation with other persons at times of change or crisis. Therefore the teacher requires a sensitivity in this area and in particular must have a conscious command of the register he uses in confronting his classes and understand the reasons for his selection at any given time. It is dangerous in any teaching situation to employ the 'I'm telling you' register too often – in drama situations it is suicidal. What of teacher as catalyst? (When I switch on the red light 'it' has begun.) As reassurer? (Don't worry, put yourself in my hands.) As devil's advocate? (That's surely not true). As good listener? (Good idea, what happens then?)

Register is related to authority and impact, and all teachers require to know which authority they dare not or cannot forego at any price. The teacher with a range of kinds of authority and ways of asserting them can employ them to serve the needs of the various classes rather than his own, and will obviously be more flexible. Our secondary and comprehensive schools demand this flexibility, and the timetabling which usually operates demands a speedy variation also. The teacher of drama can employ this for conscious effect. (i) *The authority of role.* 'I have my river pilots' licence and I am empowered by law to escort this boat and crew to the harbour bar.' (ii) *The one who knows.* 'When you've decided what you require I'll help you to find out about it.' (iii) *The teacher leader.* 'I'm in charge here.' (iv) The authority of being in a position to switch roles, to run with the hare and hunt with the hounds. Children rarely consider that they could also do this!

For me the most secure authority has always been from within the drama situation rather than the teaching one – the authority of role. Not only can I be more flexible in the use of registers, but I fear the teacher authority because I mistrust my ability to cope with a situation which may arise of teacher *against* class. The role-authority gives me shifting power and a variety of register to be at the service of the class. I may suddenly gather authority to deny or accede to requests, or be minus power but have strong opinions or to resist a class in order to strengthen its opinions and decisions. My belief in my attitudes supports their belief in theirs, but this type of teaching takes courage at first and is always a calculated risk.

A further facet of the authority spectrum is that of status and stature. Teachers who 'can be wrong' are likely to last longer and go further! This question of status is the most basic question of all, and requires concern when we train teachers, not only for drama, though because drama brings the child's subjective life into the classroom the problems of status and stature are thrown up very quickly and the teacher requires support and preparation to deal with them.

So much for the thresholds. How does drama function as an educational medium? Improvisation is essentially living at life-rate, in the present, with agreement to pretence. Dramatic activities are concerned with crisis, the experiences of life, small or large, which cause people to reflect and take note. It functions via these disciplines. The role-taker draws upon all his previous relevant experience, all his information, factual and subjective, his abilities, failings, blind-spots and skills, his character and his personality. Thus when studying and seeking to understand the 'pretend' situation he draws all relevant information to the surface and forefront *and puts it into action* but interacting with others who are also in the same situation. The important difference between life and this make-believe life is that in the latter there is the opportunity for one problem to be faced at a time with consequent selectivity being possible, and of course for different permutations of response to be tried. As stated before, it is prejudice which usually emerges first and often at first this is reinforced. I believe the teacher must accept this hazard, in any case not all prejudices are bad, but also be prepared to do something about it in due course. However the first drama discipline for the teacher is to accept the present condition of the group as revealed by their work. A group of boys chose to rob a securi-car bringing to their work all their notions about the police, property, wilful damage and right and wrong. No one was arrested even though the police-man saw the robbery – it was not in their present range to give the police the stronger hand even though their present real condition (living in an approved school!) was living testimony to the true position. As teacher I saw no point at all in forcing the issue, other than offering a mild challenge to the authenticity of the situation, for groups must forge their own truths for themselves. The sculptor and painter work via external materials, the truth of which they presently reveal. Others to a certain extent may share this truth for the materials remain to be consulted. The role-taker's material is himself and can never be static or perfect. It is therefore essential in educational drama that the teacher be skilled in helping to reveal the presently emergent truth to the group creating it.

Another natural law is that the statement must be achieved in the present and it must be seen to occur, therefore the personalities must behave at life-rate, though as stated before, there will be degrees of selectivity depending upon the skill and sensitivity of the group performing those acts and saying those words which would be relevant to the situation, and period in time, and as in life show no future or advance knowledge of what will occur as a result of those actions. All too often we plan the immediacy of the moment right out of the picture so that persons can never be confronted by themselves. We plan so that everyone knows what he ought to do next, whereas in fact we should plan so that he discovers what he *did* do next. The element of surprise is one of the most important bases of work in educational drama.

For classroom purposes the values of drama seem to me to be these: it is sociologically based, employing individuals within groups and the interaction of their active processes. It is also play-based, having a defined area of intention (as in games – a football team knows it will not end up playing at darts!) and employing elaboration. We often deny our classes elaboration time, in fact it is often taken away by the teacher's own worry or impatience. ('Finish it in ten minutes'. 'You're taking too long over that'.) Elaboration experience probably contributes more than anything else to the process of becoming a mature person. The rules of drama are definite but they are so infinitely flexible and basic that they offer a very wide range of elaboration. In football the brilliant player 'plays' his rules to their limit and good drama experience is as concerned with its rules as with the exploitation of them. So improvisation is really an elaboration procedure which employs all relevant knowledge to this date – factual and emotional information – and tests it in action. It gives immediate feedback to release energy for more elaboration because it is what Harold Rugg in *Imagination*[1] calls 'A gigantic working model'. Theatre itself is a game of elaboration within a strict framework of intent. In a sense theatre and improvisation begin at the same point. When a group of minds come together to work on the problem there is already available within them the finished product (whatever 'finish' may mean, depending upon aim) but as yet all is obscure and cloudy because the avenues by which it may be expressed and brought into focus are not yet open. If I say to a group of children 'What is a good play?' all of their answer is there available but avenues have to be opened to get the processes of elaboration working to take away the cloud so that they may perceive their answer. We then have, as in the theatre, the brilliant sparkling detail of matter which is related to the present capacities of that class. In theatre the author defines the area of intent and certain of the procedures which must be followed, e.g. words to be spoken, order of events and especially the process by which the problem will be exposed and resolved. Some plays make us aware of their aims by deliberately emphasizing the *difference* in persons, others by style, some by the words spoken. Some achieve it via surprising and shocking the audience, others by

[1] Harold Rugg, *Imagination*, Harper Row, 1963.

absurdity. In educational drama, it is the awareness of the class creating the play that we want to stimulate. In order to do this we create an opportunity for a collection of attitudes to relate together in problem-solving. All the attitudes available in the group can provide the spectrum for solving the problem, thus as a result there is opportunity for a 'widening' sphere of attitudes to be experienced, a widening appreciation of scales and numbers of problems and therefore a greater number of relationships and associations with the experiences of others to be brought into orbit and made available to the group. This is not a teaching process in the conventional sense. It comes about by a series of confrontations between persons and their ideas. The game provides the safe framework for such confrontations.

One of the reasons why teachers may experience a feeling of failure in using these procedures is that they either do not understand or fail to perceive the initial phenomena of group inertia. A group of persons gathered together, facing another person generate a kind of inertia of expectancy, and look to the one isolated person (the teacher) to solve it. We must consciously train our teachers not only to expect it as a natural phenomena but to deal with it fruitfully and at least cost to themselves. After all, the average teacher faces it a considerable number of times each day so must learn to 'carry it lightly'. The first element in solving this group-inertia problem is that of having a wide range of focus to offer. The group must become focused in order that they may begin their work. Out of this focus can emerge that moment of arrested attention which launches that work. So the teacher projects his energy firstly to focus attention, then to direct it toward the defined area of intent. It is at this stage that the teacher must know the size of groups, spaces and other risk areas he is prepared to cope with at this moment, for in defining the area with his class he can at the same time create the active situation with which he may cope. To clarify this let us take an ordinary classroom situation which often arises. We will define the teacher's thresholds as thus.

Space – he *has* only a classroom with moveable but not stackable desks. He *prefers* a hall.

Noise – A teacher on one side of his classroom prefers *not* to hear his dramatic work! He tries to respect this and anyway worries a bit himself if the children begin talking or moving rather freely.

Decisions – He prefers to plan but is learning to risk just a tiny bit. However as yet he always introduces the idea they will work on.

Size of group – He prefers children to work in groups of about five but his classroom makes this rather a difficult feat and this he is aware of.

Teaching registers – He likes to be friendly but the children know the voice of authority which appears when they take too much into their own hands. For example he will always prevent a 'fight' developing, see it 'a mile off' and deflect it, unless he can plan it and know in advance (*a*) who will win, (*b*) how many will take active part, and (*c*) what all the others will be doing. The class is a group of lively ten year olds – equally divided between boys and girls.

Understanding of the medium – He realizes the significance of selecting a problem. He is not yet good at or swift in helping children's own ideas to take the lead but he wants this to happen and he recognizes the extra quality present in work where ideas and disciplines are acquired together.

Subject chosen – The Easter Story (*a*) because it might be pleasant to 'work it up' for the other classes to see (*b*) He knows it is exciting, especially the entry into Jerusalem, The Last Supper, the arrest in the garden of Gethsemane, the trial and Peter's denial and finally the carrying of the cross (and he is right!) He sees that the material is relevant to girls *and* boys but he doesn't wish to foist a heavily moral viewpoint upon them.

Now, remember, he has as yet no space, he doesn't wish to make much noise, he doesn't want the children to become too excited yet he *does* want to use this theme and initially with smallish groups. So he must find first a focus which is relevant to boys and girls so that attention will be arrested. Because he wishes to work with small groups he immediately, before he even opens his mouth, must have decided whether mixed-sex groups will be chosen by him, or whether he will allow the boys and girls to select their own groupings and if he does this he knows in advance that his groups will be composed of either all boys or all girls! So *that* must be settled before he decides that the time has come when girls and boys must start working in mixed small groups. He therefore must examine his theme to find a focus which requires mixed small groups. *Any* theme will yield problems to suit *any* type and condition of class. These immediately leap to my mind if one looks at the Easter Story: families out in the evening in the Garden witness the arrest, groups of soldiers and women at the well during the entry into Jerusalem, witnesses of the trial spotting Peter and accusing him; a disciple's family at *any* of these events, the room below that in which the last supper takes place with women preparing food and disciples occasionally entering to collect and return dishes and to report. It can readily be seen that because of his group size and noise thresholds, most of the conventional visions of the Easter story must be bypassed. This is not necessarily a disadvantage but he must be extremely flexible in conjuring up small group areas to be explored. He will be at a distinct advantage in using small groups to explore some of the personal agonies, fears, and bewilderments arising out of the larger panorama of events, but he *cannot* do these large panoramic events, because he has 'cut his crowd scenes' by sacking his actors. All of the small group scenes mentioned however (and there will be hundreds of others within the theme – what of Joseph of Arimathea? Did *his* family welcome the idea of a notorious stranger occupying their beautifully constructed tomb?), may provide a nucleus of experiences which may be then fed into the larger panoramic view and this can be another advantage to him. All his desks can be easily utilized for any of these small-group ideas.

So before he meets his class he must already have examined his theme to discover the size and intensity of his small group problems. He then must present his theme via focus upon 'family' situations. For example should he choose to focus attention by using a picture, say of the entry into Jerusalem or The Last Supper, he must *not* discuss the crowd situations. Instead he must lead immediately into study of smaller 'kin' groupings (e.g. friends, families, shared feelings) otherwise his focus will be irrelevant to the development he can afford to permit. He has created for himself one enormous problem which, if he does not realize it, will cause all the work to be hard graft instead of a pleasurable exciting evolving of ideas gradually crystallizing into form. This problem is, that because he has chosen small groups he is placing an emphasis upon language in the main, and to a certain extent upon the more subtle relationships and emotions. His ten year old class may be at a loss to do more than touch the fringe of these problems, and he and they may be disappointed and frustrated. One of the early tasks of the teacher is to create experiences of intensity (not necessarily of depth) because these are the ones which will commit the class to further work as they give instant success feedback. Only the teacher can ensure that no failure is experienced – the group cannot. It is at once simpler and more economical to achieve this for the whole class. Looking at our Easter story again, which are the moments when intense experiences may be easily created? Usually these are easiest and most powerful when all the group are focused upon one, for example a crowd watching a Christ carrying an obviously too heavy cross will have a reaction; whether it is obvious or not is irrelevant. A crowd watching a soldier taking a crown of thorns, pass it amongst them then place it upon the head of Christ cannot avoid a kind of involvement though it may be inactive, a crowd of happy citizens suddenly hearing the voices or marching feet of troops in the garden in the evening will have their attention arrested even momentarily. If our teacher understands this, he will naturally see that tensions of this nature are within his small group situations. It can readily be seen now that his material of focus, whether spoken, seen, handled, or heard must have this element in it. Strangely enough this experience element is the one most often omitted, yet this is the very experience which will release energy to get further similar experiences.

A further tool in the hands of our teacher will be his ability to employ a flexible range of linguistic registers. He does *not* require to be an actor or a vocal sensation with hundreds of dialects and accents in his repertoire but he does require to indicate attitudes, different stratas in society, periods and style, by his own choice of words, tone, pitch and pause when he makes his contribution. Remember we do not ask of the children that they shall act only in the stage actor sense, only that they shall take up attitudes and viewpoints and for the time believe in them. Ability in this area gives the teacher the opportunity to become one with the class because he can without apparent effort select words which are in the children's own register, put them at their ease or draw their attention if that is necessary. The odd curse, and cutting off of consonants, together with a slight roughening of tone have 'saved my bacon' often in the early stages when working with tough town boys. A variety of registers is also essential for helping groups to capture mood, quality and type of tension, social strata of personnel, period and style, *provided it is a hint and not a performance!*

c

Lastly it can be employed to put in a press toward further development of the group by advancing them into less well-known and understood territory and a deeper consideration of the situation.

If we again look at our Easter Story situation, the teacher will conduct his early discussions in rather different idioms if his class is from the stockbroker belt than if it is in a down-town area, and also his 'Joseph of Arimathea' family require a different verbal register feed than that given to a poor fisherman's family watching the struggle to Calvary. Please understand this is not to suggest that our teacher becomes a chameleon or a mountebank, only that he can indicate verbal changes (sometimes crudely, sometimes slightly). I recall an extremely bright class of forty-two top juniors living on an ice planet called Isagon developing an original verbal style in keeping with their culture because as their leader I slightly stressed the 'S' sounds in words. This was taken up by them and gave rise to a whole new conception of motor development. We travelled via a type of hover-system and it arose entirely from the slight sibilance of my words.

The last important linguistic area is that of knowing (a) what not to say and (b) when not to speak – the hardest area of all. This is only achieved when the teacher is so secure that all his attention, except that necessary area of detachment which is his teaching life-line, is focused upon the working group and not upon his own image and status.

So we focus, then we define our area, then we elaborate and out of elaboration comes the next stage: the demand, which I believe is basic in all human beings, for form to be achieved. Again it is the teacher's responsibility to perceive when a press towards form may be made, and at what level that form may be achieved. A class of six-year-olds making a tournament achieved form by ordering the events, the places in which the events would happen, the processions to and from, the winner's and loser's prizes and the harmony of the head-dresses of the ladies. This was 'doing' form. A class of fourteen-year-olds, working on the voices of the Sybil in the cave, worked entirely on juxtaposing and texturing sound-effects. Form in educational work must be achieved in conjunction with the needs of the class.

What is form? Like drama, we all understand it when it happens. The first component would appear to be the ordering of the miscellaneous and reducing miscellany to order. In drama this miscellany is all the variety of life experience available in the group, and their range of ideas for solutions to the current problems, all their differing ways of approach (whether convergent or divergent), and the way they actually perceive their work. Elaboration reveals the miscellany.

The second ingredient would appear to be a process of simplification. In *Imagination* Harold Rugg notes, 'The essence of creative activity lies in a simplifying process which automatically involves not only the selection and rearrangement of the available material but its modification in process of developing a simpler form'.[1] Louis Danz says, 'Form is that kind of organization to which nothing can be added and from which nothing can be taken'.[2]

Thirdly form is 'fitness of purpose' of all the material contained in it. Form making is not a process of finishing something, it is a forward moving procedure constantly simplifying, seeing more clearly. It is not a static repetition for we can never exactly repeat an experience: would it be worthwhile?

So in the creative work we have focus, definition, elaboration and form. There is a further area – that of maturation and casting off. Maturation in educational terms seems to me to be 'the total end possible at this present time'. Some creative work can be preserved and daily lived with, met freshly and re-savoured over and over again, clay pots, short stories, paintings, recorded music, fabrics, and though this can be naturally cast-off in favour of other visions, it is not a lost thing but a no-longer needed one. A positive casting off is a feature of living, and in the drama field it may take many forms. Showing to others, humbly or with great style, is the most often used. Sometimes however the material achievement is such that it requires to be written up as a record (for example the third year remove class of girls working on a drama of 'How to select a husband' decided to create an advice column as the end product), crystallized into economical film, developed into a series of lectures[3] (the 1st year girls grammar school class dramatizing the development of Christianity in Northumberland decided that they had too much material for a play!)

I have dealt with what I believe to be the fundamental areas we

[1] Harold Rugg, *Imagination*, Harper Row 1963.
[2] Louis Danz, *The Psychologist Looks at Art*, New York: Longmans 1937, p. 80.
[3] Written up as a book or a miscellany of thoughts and reflections upon the play made rather than showing the play to others. These are only a few.

should be considering if we are to help teachers to employ drama creatively in school: to confront their thresholds in basic drama 'rules' in the classroom, and now finally to choose material to use in relation to age and ability levels in classes. Good material serves all classes and circumstances. One selects an *area* of the material upon which to work which serves the needs of the children All material will be concerned with 'people, now'. Variations will be used depending upon the strata in society, and the verbal, emotional development and imagination of the class. Harold Rugg again in *Imagination* says:

> the principal function of imagination is to enable the human being constantly to build thought models of the real world. The inventor conceives in imagination new arrangements of his machine-parts to bring about described movements. The creative dancer conceives in imagination the right movements for the objectification of his or her imagined conception. The mathematician imagines alternative hierarchies of symbols of relationship. Recall Einstein's never-ending task of imagining 'what would happen if . . . one were to run after a beam of light or ride on one . . . if you could run fast enough . . . would you reach a point where it would not move at all?' Or the imaginative work in Cezanne's perception-in-depth of the strong hidden skeleton beneath the surface of his valley landscape.
>
> The steps involved in thinking point to the crucial role of the imagination: the capacity to delay responses; to manipulate symbols in imagination; to sense and hold the direction dictated by perception and recall; and to generalize, that is, to form and use concepts. Much of our thinking is done by imagined body movements. A little boy in Lincoln School's first grade said, 'I can't say it, but I can draw it.' A four-year-old girl said, 'Mummy, I'll dance it, you write it.' The chief distinction between men and animals is this capacity to work out solutions to problems symbolically, in imagination. To use Koestler's phrasing, 'Artists treat facts as stimuli for imagination, whereas scientists use imagination to coordinate facts.'

I find the best kind of guide to help me in considering material is (i) a short basic list: Drive (what makes a group want to do something); Feedback (what satisfactions are achieved by doing it); Signals (the range of communication within the group); and Rituals (the experiences which seem to be required to be made again and again – individual and group) and finally Content (the level at which children can work). A list of the areas into which culture may be divided: work, war, education, health, food, family, shelter, travel, communication, clothing, worship, law and leisure (I realize there are other groupings equally relevant). *All* material yields some aspect of all these and all classes will find some excitement and relevance in one or other of them. The more flexibly the teacher can learn to approach material the better, if only to achieve constant rejuvenation rather than deprivation of himself and his ideas. If we look at this list it is easy to see that some areas are more obviously 'beginner's areas' than others, able to be achieved with less subtlety of design, making fewer verbal or emotional demands. For example 'worship' in drama can cover a range from a personal silent prayer to the most complex academic argument on the church's philosophy. It is a matter of the teacher finding the level and area which will stretch a class yet give satisfaction in those five areas of the first list.

So it would appear that in helping teachers we require to devise situations free of tension which will enable them to define their present teaching needs threshold-wise, to understand as well as they may precisely what makes drama 'tick', to be flexible in selecting, presenting and handling their material and to observe honestly their teaching results. Obviously the operative words in the above sentence are 'free of tensions' so value judgements and relationships concerned with status are not relevant here. Until we can train so that the end-product is open to receiving positively staff and classroom experiences, teachers will go on teaching behind the closed doors of their classrooms. This means that teachers must be (i) able to discover and healthily recognize their real strengths and also to understand that strengths and positive qualities embody their darker sides – punctuality in a person can make him intolerant of others who are less time conscious for example; (ii) to teach as much by intake from their classes as by output to them; (iii) to forgive themselves for their failures and start afresh; (iv) to *structure* (in terms of 'Build') their drama lessons rather than plan the children's contribution out of them and so spend precious time trying to keep to the plan; (v) to observe clearly what is really happening as the children dramatize; and lastly (vi) to bring to school not only their information. This way the realness in the teacher can keep alive and present the realness in the children.

Included in almost all our recent statements of aspiration in education – to educate more scientists and more mathematicians, to teach more foreign languages, to produce well-disciplined, nondelinquent, responsible citizens – are diatribes directed against the school system by professors in liberal arts colleges, irate parents, high military officers, public speakers, but they seldom go to the heart of the matter, and that is the chance we give teachers to teach.

The truth of the matter is that it is not *teachers* we look down on, fail to value, fail to reward – it is *teaching* itself.

MORE THAN LIP SERVICE

Medicine is an art regarded with reverence. Why should the ability to stimulate and shape a well mind be less valued than the surgical skill to remove a tumour from a damaged one? This is itself a measure of our present lip service to creativity. We want people who are original, creative, spontaneous, innovative. But we want them to be produced by teachers whom we condemn in a hundred ways to be overworked and uninspired, unrespected and underpaid. We have seen what a related activity has done in the arts where we overvalue the product while we undervalue the living painter, allowing him to starve or to eke out a miserable living with commercial art, while we auction off the works of his comfortable dead predecessor for $100,000 a painting. So, also, we would like the children of America – as a product – to be creative, to learn about creativity, while we make the best chance they have to learn, to respond to teaching, as uncreative as possible.

There is only one sure way to develop creativity in all the different kinds of children in our schools. We must cherish all the way through – in the normal school and the teachers' college, in the way the teacher's job is set up, in the freedom granted to the teacher to teach while others perform the thousand chores which are no essential part of this task and this art, in the time given the teacher to read and explore and think and plan and search for new materials – the creativity of all those who have elected to become teachers because they want to teach.

If we are to give more than lip service to creativity in children, we must actively support the creativity of the teacher. That is to say, we must come to recognize fully the creativity of good teaching.[1]

[1] Ross Mooney and Tahir Razik (Eds.), *Explorations in Creativity,* Harper Row.

4. Movement as a Preparation for Drama

Veronica Sherborne

I THINK everyone would agree that if you want to acquire a skill of any kind, whether playing the piano or swimming, it is essential to learn through doing. When this is not practicable the next best thing is to see others learning. So for the Clifton College Conference I decided to take a class to illustrate my ideas about movement as a preparation for acting, and I hoped the audience would find the subject interesting enough to wish to pursue it further. In attempting to communicate the experience of movement in words I shall inevitably lose some of its essential qualities. Movement is dynamic, ephemeral, often spontaneous, and the teaching of it requires a sensitive rapport between teacher and class. The class must be fun, as well as instructive; to move well requires intelligence and imagination; the whole personality is involved, both body and mind.

The students who took part in the class were experienced and confident in movement, which was necessary as they were working on a stage in front of a large audience. They came from four different institutions. Six of the men were studying either in the Drama Department of Bristol University, the Bristol Old Vic Theatre School or at Redland College of Education. The six women students and one man were from the National Association for Mental Health Course for teachers of mentally handicapped children. As a part-time tutor on this course I had worked with them for nearly two years, with the main emphasis on teaching.

None of these men and women students had worked in this particular group before, and part of my plan was to show how simply and quickly one could use different relationships in movement terms to help people work sensitively and creatively together.

During the class I worked on three aspects of movement which I consider are fundamentally important to anyone who wants to move expressively. My main objective is to build up self-confidence through developing physical, or bodily, confidence, and as a result of this to encourage people to become more expressive and creative. I explained briefly to the audience how I had come to think as I do. For the last ten years I have been working with student teachers of mentally handicapped children. These children may have the body of a twelve-year-old, but function in many ways like a child of two or three. Most of these children have limited, or non-existent speech, and find the inability to communicate through speech very frustrating. Communication through movement is therefore particularly necessary for them, and I have noticed how much normal children also benefit from using movement as a way of expressing themselves. There are two things here: one can use movement as a way of making contact with other people, and as a non-verbal way of expressing something about oneself.

In my work with mentally handicapped children I have noticed how the children have little or no sense of awareness of their bodies. When they are encouraged to become aware of their knees, feet, their hands, and perhaps of their bodies as a whole, they become more aware of themselves. They can be helped to develop a stronger sense of being a person, they can discover some sense of identity. I have observed this developing self-awareness in normal children, in students, in teachers, and in actors, and part of my programme is to work on strengthening self-awareness through increasing bodily awareness.

I have also noticed how much mentally handicapped children and normal children get from what I can only call developing a good relationship to the ground. Movement close to the floor can give a sense of security and confidence. It is a help to everyone to become more aware, not only of his own attitude to weight and gravity, but of the many aspects of relating to these which exist. In pursuing this I notice that people become much more 'earthed', more aware of themselves, and more secure. I notice how much people need the experience of being well-earthed and well-centred, and how helpful this can be in dramatic work of all kinds. My concern with awareness of oneself, and awareness of others, has developed because this awareness and understanding is so often limited, and people are prevented from achieving their best because of these limitations.

AWARENESS OF OTHERS

Many of the students in this class did not know each other. I asked them first of all to take a partner they did know, to put their hands on their partner's shoulders and push, and see who was the stronger, who had the most determination. Each person is testing his strength against his partner. The struggle is humorous and good-natured, the ice is broken and a vigorous start is made. I asked the students to find another partner, someone they did not know, and work against this person. It is interesting to compare different kinds of attack and resistance in different partners, and to be aware of the great variety of ways of expressing these. The students changed partners, and tried out other ways of pushing, shoulder to shoulder, hip against hip, back against back. They also tried pulling their partners, holding wrists. When working recently with an autistic boy I noticed he refused to push against his partner, but he enjoyed pulling and tugging away from him. It may be easier for some to start with pulling, as pushing is such an outspoken statement of being involved with another person. I have never found children or adolescents hurt each other in these mock fights, but where one person is much bigger or stronger he will adapt his strength to his partner. One can develop this adapt- ation to a partner's strength into a slow motion fight or wrestling match where first one person is allowed to overcome, and then the other. This calls for a sensitive adjustment of tension and a great deal of concentration.

The students put so much energy into these trials of strength that we could not continue for as long as a class of beginners might. The more experienced students can focus their attention and call up all their energy more quickly and effectively than the beginners can. The concentration on strength comes more easily to boys on the whole, and they seem to find total involvement easier than girls do. The main strength in working against another person comes from the thrust of the legs against the ground. It is valuable to develop this kind of strength, to be able to stand your ground, and to be self-assertive. The teacher should be prepared for a varying amount of noise during this activity; it is a normal and sometimes necessary initial reaction. When the class has used up some of its energy, they are then ready for a more considerate and careful way of relating to a partner.

I asked the students to find a new partner, to hold his wrists, to sit back a little, and balance each other's weight. The dialogue here is no longer *against* one another, but a communication of mutual trust. The students tried many ways of balancing the weight of a partner, see-saws, spinning round, sinking and rising while spinning; they leant back to back and tried sitting down and rising while leaning against each other, and many other variations.

The students then took the whole of their partner's weight for a brief moment, helping each other to jump. The partner tried jumping straight up, and round their supporter, with flying legs. One partner sat, or lay, on the ground, and the other pulled him off the floor with a flying jump, helping him to experience flight for a moment.

We then tried different ways of taking the entire weight of the partner. One of the pair knelt on all fours, and the other draped himself backwards, or forwards, over his partner's back. One partner picked up the other in a fireman's lift. The students stood back to back, linked elbows, one bent forward lifting the other on to his back. The one being lifted tried to relax as much as possible, and had to be able to trust his supporting partner completely. All these balancings, liftings, supportings demand mutual trust and confidence, and with each change of partner, different degrees of these are experienced. Some people find it difficult to commit themselves to the care of another person. These activities are best carried out in a relaxed and humorous atmosphere, and anxiety and tension can be lessened.

By this point the students were beginning to feel more confident and at ease with each other. They were sufficiently involved in what they were doing to be able sometimes to forget the audience. Working with a partner in an objective and practical way helps beginners to be less self-conscious. We then tried out awareness of others in groups of three, a further development of 'against' another, and 'with' another. Two people held a 'prisoner' between them, holding an elbow and hand firmly. The prisoner appeared to be struggling free, but in fact was moving in the most mobile and flexible way while relying on the support of his two companions. The two supporters held the middle person while he writhed and struggled, and he was able to move much more freely because of their support. This experience is particularly helpful in getting people to move from the hips, and to bend back. When everyone had had a turn in the middle the students tried a trusting exercise where one person stands between two supporters, and falls towards one of them. This person catches him on the shoulders and gently pushes him towards the other supporter. The middle person falls passively, but not limply, from side to side, or forwards and backwards. If someone is nervous about falling, or is particularly heavy, the two catchers can stand behind him and each catch him under an arm. It is a good idea to begin by falling only just out of the vertical, and then increase the fall gradually.

I find that a person who has confidence in himself is more likely to have confidence in others, and by using these activities I have seen trust and confidence grow. Sometimes I say to a class, 'Two of you plck up the third, carry him off and put him down somewhere eise.' It is amusing to see the variety of ways of carrying which are found. The one who is to be carried can present his lifters with a problem, a limp body, a rigid one, a tight ball, and so on.

A third way of helping people to become more aware of others is much less physically strenuous, and requires sensitivity and delicacy. I find this quality of sensitivity is more deeply experienced when it comes as a contrast to the strong physical interactions I have described. I asked the students to lead their partners by one hand, or both, guiding them forward, backward, turning, travelling, moving gently and slowly, and giving the partner time to respond to the messages coming through his hands. The one who is being led will be more aware of these indications to rise, sink, turn, etc., if he shuts his eyes and feels himself being carefully and gently directed. It is valuable to change partners and so become more aware of the many different ways of guiding and responding.

For this sensitive interplay music of the right kind can heighten the quality of fine touch and sense of taking care of someone. Sometimes I use very delicate Japanese music, sometimes a slow movement from a Bach Concerto, sometimes a folk song. The students then tried guiding their partners through light touch on the shoulders, elbows, chin, back, waist, so that the partner was almost moulded like a piece of clay. Then one partner folded and wrapped the other into a ball, rocked and cradled this person, and then unfolded the partner slowly until he was opened out.

I would normally work on this theme of awareness of others throughout a class, developing it into imaginative interplays where physical contact was no longer used. After a class has experienced different ways of relating to partners in a physical way, they remain sensitive and aware of others when there is no actual contact, and the most inspired and imaginative improvisation comes at this point. In building towards expressive and imaginative work it helps to prepare the ground first by developing an awareness and acceptance of others. The frequent changes of partner help a group of individuals to accept each other more readily. Work in twos, threes, and fours will contribute to sensitive interactions when the group is larger. The kind of groundwork I have described, can contribute towards the working out of relationships within a plan, and it makes actors more aware of how relationships can be expressed through movement. Instead of developing this theme of awareness of others to its artistic conclusion, I went back to the beginning again, introducing a second theme which has a basic contribution to make to the skill of acting.

AWARENESS OF THE GROUND

This kind of awareness involves a coming to terms with the weight of the body, an awareness of one's body against the ground, and the experience of the ground as a support and a base from which to move. A person's attitude to his weight and to the ground shows clearly in his walk. It is helpful to an actor to be aware of his own natural way of standing, sitting, and walking, and to experience many other ways which could enrich his understanding and portraying of people very different from himself. The first thing to do is to experience what it is to be anchored, or earthed. The students lay on their faces or on their backs, and found out how they could move over the floor, shifting, wriggling, rolling, sliding. A clean, slightly slippery, floor is essential here. Working on the floor gives people a greater awareness of their bodies against the hard surface, they can move more freely and flexibly close to the ground than when standing up and balance is a problem. The support of the floor is similar to that of water, something of the same kind of freedom can be experienced in working on the ground as is felt while swimming. An element of self-trust can be observed in the way people move over the floor. Some people are nervous about letting their weight be carried, and this shows mainly in the head, which is not allowed to rest on the floor. I have very occasionally taught an emotionally disturbed child who would not even sit on the floor.

I asked the students to roll stretched out, to roll curled up, and then to change from one to the other, feeling the impulse to move coming very much from the centre of the body. The students tried rolling on to shoulders, on to their sides, their hips, their knees; they crawled close to the floor, backwards and forwards; they linked together crawling and rolling. Inevitably these contractings and spreadings, slitherings and crawlings, remind one of snakes, insects, amoeba, tigers, and are much enjoyed by children. The students then practised falling, starting from kneeling. A partner gave them a push, they fell softly over and rose up on their knees again, allowing the momentum of the fall to take them. Letting the body go is accompanied by a mental letting go, an allowing of the body to move by itself. Awareness of the body against the ground helps people to become more relaxed, more flexible, and more at home in their bodies. Some of these movements are a re-discovery of methods of locomotion enjoyed in early childhood. They come a little hard on the adult who has developed all kinds of tensions and is not as rubbery as he was. The element of child's play in all these activities is quite helpful to the actor. The next step was to stand on two feet, squatting close to the floor, and to walk about with these very short legs. The ability to move about very close to the ground is demonstrated by Chinese actors and Balinese dancers, who seem to flow over the floor quite effortlessly. From being very short, the students slowly stretched their legs as if discovering them for the first time. They stamped and squashed, and thudded on the floor, playing with the weight of the body against the ground. I like to use music with a strong beat to accompany rhythmical stampings and beatings, stressing movement downwards with a lot of strength.

The connection between feet and the floor can be developed in a myriad of ways, but I stress the anchoring and earthing experiences until I feel the group have got this into their systems. Then one can explore shuffling, sliding, gliding, barely touching the floor, using it as a springboard, pouncing on it, being weightless and airborne, and so on.

AWARENESS OF ONESELF

The first two themes I have described are also valuable ways of developing self-awareness, but the acquiring of this may be indirect. In the first two themes everyone has something to work with, either another person, or the ground, but in this third theme one is alone with oneself. I have relied on learning through the sense of touch a great deal in the first two themes, and here again the sense of touch can help one to become more aware of oneself. The students began by banging their knees, holding on to them while they walked, turned, and jumped. They pressed their knees back, pushed them forward, knocked them together. Children benefit particularly from experiencing the hardness and aliveness of different parts of the body through feeling and contact. Knees can be very expressive and comic, and the audience found the students' improvisations very entertaining. The students then worked on their hips, often a very immobile part of the body. Because the legs and hips are used for weight bearing and loco-motion it is hard for people to become aware of how expressive they can be. In the beginning it seems more important to develop the mastery and sensitive control of the centre and the legs than of the upper half of the body. If the centre of the body is dead, then all movement will look empty, and will feel empty. By concentrating on one part of the body at a time one can discover the expressive potential of different parts, the back, shoulders, elbows, wrists, fingers, neck, head, face and eyes. The body is an expressive instrument, and to play an instrument well, one must be able to play all the notes. One must not forget the need to move the body as a harmonious whole, because finally one wants to integrate the person. Moving from the centre is perhaps the hardest control to achieve, but when people have learnt to move from the centre, their movement seems to belong to them, and they move in an integrated way.

The teacher needs to be very bodily aware himself to teach this aspect of movement well. In the beginning the movement will be large, exaggerated, and sometimes a caricature. As the class gains greater skill, movement can become more refined, more economic, more subtle, more telling. The greatest economy in movement I have seen is in the Noh theatre of Japan, where the smallest movements become increasingly significant to the viewer, and where one is made more aware of the value of stillness.

The students finished their strenuous session with improvising in threes in different ways; two dominating one, one dominating two, all three meeting and parting with the emphasis on simplicity, and other interplays. The applause at the end indicated how much the audience had appreciated their concentrated energy, their inventiveness, wit, and sensitivity.

The activities I have described form a useful, and, I think, essential preparation for dramatic work. There are, however, many other aspects of movement which the teacher or producer needs to understand. Perhaps the most important ingredient of movement is that which gives colour to movement, *how* a movement is performed. Observing the quality of movement, and knowing all the variations of quality which exist will help the producer to clarify and sharpen the way a movement is performed. Although not specifically mentioned, this aspect of movement was inherent in everything the students did in their class. It is helpful to stress the extremes of movement quality in the beginning, to contrast strength with delicacy, speed and suddenness with sustainment and calmness. Movement which is very controlled is contrasted with spontaneous and abandoned movement, movement which is economic in its use of space (linear and one dimensional) is contrasted with a more extravagant use of space (flexible and three dimensional). Awareness of energy, time, flow of movement, and the use of space can give the actor a rich movement language. He will be more conscious of how he moves, of the dramatic impact of the extremes of movement quality, and the content of what he is doing will be much clearer.

How the material is communicated to the class is especially important in movement teaching. The relationship between the teacher and class will affect the quality of the work achieved. Creative work demands mutual respect between teacher and taught. The teacher will know the ground the class needs to cover, but how this is done, and how it is developed will depend on the response of the group. The teacher will be improvising on a theme, and what emerges will be a dialogue between teacher and class, a shared experience. A great deal of the content of the class will come from the group, and the teacher needs to be on the look-out for contributions which will take the group further. The group will feel satisfied, extended, and involved inasmuch as the teacher has valued and used their contributions. It is comparatively easy to teach exercises, and to impose one's own style on to a group. It is harder to develop the potential of a class, so that each individual does not imitate the teacher, but develops his own resources with the teacher's help.

I have contributed as a movement adviser and choreographer to many productions, and have been fortunate to work with a number of producers. I prefer to work with a cast from the start of rehearsals, helping them to find the right style which is the essence of a play, and helping individual actors to discover the right physical feel and expression for their parts. In my experience when a cast works from a sound movement basis from the beginning, the final production benefits enormously. The proper understanding and use of movement can give an actor a rich movement vocabulary, and it can heighten and intensify dramatic experience.

My approach to movement is a personal one, worked out over many years. It has grown from what I first learned from Rudolf Laban. Everyone has to find his or her own way of working, and I offer some of my findings to those who are also exploring. I do not suggest a 'method', but I would like to share an approach with teachers and producers who may find something here which might be useful to them.

RECOMMENDED FILMS

In Touch. Movement for mentally handicapped children. Made for Veronica Sherborne by Drama Department, University of Bristol. Concord Films Council, Nacton, Ipswich, Suffolk.
Explorations. An approach to movement for drama. By Veronica Sherborne, and available from Concord Films Council, Nacton, Ipswich, Suffolk.
Chinese Theatre. National Audio-Visual Aids Library, 2 Paxton Place, Gipsy Road, London, S.E.27.

5. The School Play

John Hersee

THE SCHOOL PLAY has been the subject of many attacks. It may be valuable to list some of the features traditionally associated with a school play as a backcloth to what follows. The play is usually an annual event, whether or not talent or interest exists, involving a great upheaval in the life of the school. Probably the Assembly Hall has to be modified or rearranged to stage the play and all the lessons and other activities which normally take place there must be cancelled or moved. The audience, a mixture of adoring parents, compelled pupils and critical colleagues of the producer, pay to sit for a long time on hard school chairs, straining to see and hear – the duration of the play made even more protracted by the lengthy intervals to allow for scene changes. The play is probably Shakespeare; perhaps because of the large cast and, in a boys' school, the nature of the female parts; perhaps because the Head of English who has again been saddled with this annual burden feels at home only with this author; or perhaps because the Headmaster looks upon the School Play as a prestige venture for the school and feels that Shakespeare (or some of it) is suitable as such and distrusts any 'modern' play.

The helpers, the technicians and scene builders have laboured for weeks within an inadequate budget to try to create on the minute stage a highly realistic effect, the realism of which vanishes when the first character to enter is seen to be taller than the keep of the castle and whose shadow on the sky effectively obliterates the carefully painted clouds. For the actors there have been weeks of rehearsal and line-learning. The producer wishes that he had had more rehearsal time but realizes that he could not have faced another minute of it! Producers are of two kinds. They may be pictured as autocrats who issue precise instructions which the cast obey without daring to question, who demonstrate and 'drill' every inflection, gesture and movement. Alternatively, they are benign father-figures, with little knowledge of the techniques or crafts of the theatre, who believe that the important thing is for everyone to 'have a good act' and whose instructions are confined to telling the cast to 'speak up' and not to mask each other. In neither case is there any real discussion of character, motivation or situation, nor is there any sense of development as rehearsals proceed; the main concentration is on getting the lines learnt!

When it is all over everyone congratulates everyone else, says how marvellous it has all been and secretly whispers thanks that it is all over for another year. The scenery is broken up as there is nowhere to store it, the Hall reverts to its normal usage and everyone forgets about drama for another year.

Although this picture is a caricature it would be wrong to deny that productions have been and still are run on these lines, and we must be aware of the lost opportunities and inadequacies of such methods. It must be said at once that many of these faults and difficulties arise directly or indirectly from lack of facilities and finance; given adequate provision of both, the organization and work involved in mounting a production is still considerable, but the producer's energies can be concentrated on the play and not dispersed over many peripheral problems.

In terms of facilities the main requirements are: for the audience – comfortable seats, a good view of the stage or acting area, good acoustic conditions; for the performers and helpers – a good 'stage', good lighting equipment, good sound equipment, and adequate storage.

Many forms of 'stage' are in use at the present time and different schools may desire to experiment with the type of staging they use, but the stage must be good of its kind. For example, a proscenium stage requires adequate wing space and considerable height above the proscenium, amongst other qualities. Recommended sizes and proportions are available and architects should have no difficulty in obtaining the necessary information. In use the 'theatre' must be readily available for its primary purpose, to avoid the upheavals and difficulties mentioned, but it will provide facilities for many other activities within the school.

There are two characteristics which distinguish the activities which I shall include under this title from the dramatic activities which are the concern of the other papers. The fundamental one is that the whole venture is directed towards performance before an audience and thus essentially involves communication, not only amongst the performers themselves, but also with the audience who are outside the main action. Within a drama lesson the members of the group involved in a piece of work seek to communicate amongst themselves and thus develop a common appreciation of their subject; it is conceivable that a well-drilled production can communicate with the audience without there being any real communication or interplay between the actors as the characters they are portraying. But a true performance involves both forms of communication; unless the audience receives and understands the performance nothing is achieved and the characters in the play will only really 'live' if the actors playing them are really aware of each other *as* the characters and listen and react accordingly. All this, and especially communicating with the audience requires various skills and techniques to be learned and a generally agreed 'meaning' to be put across. The skills and techniques must not become ends in themselves but must be seen as necessary aids to effective performance.

In addition to the scripted play, which may be considered the usual form, types of performance which may be suitable include: 'rehearsed improvisation', revue, dancing, and opera.

The script of the play may be an 'accepted' text, from Sophocles to Speight or a play devised and written within the school, either by a teacher, or pupil, or by teachers and pupils together. The type of performance or play chosen will depend on many factors, important among which may well be the size of the school. There can be little doubt that those who derive the greatest benefit from a production are the performers and helpers. Thus an aim will be to arrange that as many pupils as possible have the opportunity to participate, either as actors or technicians. Some schools attempt to do this by tackling a spectacular production with a huge cast and with the backstage jobs shared out between many people. This may go some way towards achieving the aim, but cannot be considered completely successful in doing so. The parts the actors play inevitably become smaller in many cases and it is hard for the fifth spear-carrier to feel really involved. Actors with smaller parts find less stimulus and challenge in those parts and all too easily know only the scene in which they appear and nothing of the rest of the play. Similarly, the backstage helpers find themselves with less responsibility.

A much better method is to have several productions during

the school year. The selection of participants can be based on age, House, Form, Set or any other convenient unit. There may be a basic 'pattern' involving House Plays, Form plays, age-group plays, but in addition it should be possible for any group to put on a performance – perhaps based on work developed during drama lessons, perhaps as a result of textual study in literature lessons or of a play written by one or more of their number. It may still be a good idea to consider one (or more) of these productions as The School Play, chosen and directed by a teacher, staged rather more elaborately and drawing on a wider range of potential participants. The other productions may be used to exploit different types of performances, to involve different groups within the school, to give experience and training to many more pupils and to keep the work alive throughout the year in the school. It goes without saying that such a programme requires adequate facilities and the involvement of many teachers.

The second characteristic of all these activities is that generally they are based, either wholly or in part, on extra-curricular time. There are obvious exceptions to this, and varying amounts of preparation may take place in lesson time, but most rehearsals, scene-building, not to mention the performances, take place 'after school'. Craft classes may work on scenery during lessons, and Art classes may paint it, but the long continuous sessions necessary for finishing the set on stage, arranging the lights and lighting and for rehearsals which a major performance requires can only be found outside the timetable. Further, it is only at such times that all the different sections of the school, all the different talents, skills and interests, which contribute to the creation of the play and all the actors, if they are drawn from a wide range of the school, can come together. Indeed, I feel strongly that it is wrong for the 'duties' to be exclusively allocated by departments within the school so that the play is produced by the English or the Drama department, staged by the Art and Handicraft departments, lit by the Physics department with special effects by the Chemistry department and sound by the Music department. That is not to say that these departments should never make these particular contributions. But to allocate these roles exclusively in these ways again misses opportunities. We are conscious today of the dangers of over-specialization and of the narrowness that this can impose upon the pupils. It seems to me that we can do something to counteract this and to show the value of a breadth of interest if teachers involved in work upon plays take on tasks which do not seem to be immediately allied to the subjects they teach. We should make it possible for any teacher who has the necessary qualities, abilities and interest to produce a play. In this way the pupils will see aspects of the teacher's personality not usually shown in the classroom. Drama and theatre call upon the whole person as no other subject does and we should take every opportunity to express this. Thus the school play can become the meeting point of a large number of people and an activity which takes place across the divisions and barriers which the timetable creates.

Although I have suggested that several productions within the course of a school year, cast and organized in different ways, are valuable to provide as many opportunities for participants as possible, it is convenient to consider some details of a major 'School Play' production to develop this theme. The features of such a production will be shared to some degree by all other productions even though the latter may be of different types or on a different scale. In contrast to the picture presented at the beginning of this paper, we may assume that the approach of the teacher who is producing the play will be designed to develop the pupil's abilities and awareness, while ensuring that a performance that is worthy of the audience's attention results. The choice of the 'play' to be performed will be influenced by several factors. One of these will be the producer's interest in a particular script, but he will also consider the school's facilities, the performers and talents available and the interests of the participants. Any author may be considered; a play by Shakespeare may provide the best answer on some occasions but will not do so always. Whatever the choice the performers' interest and enthusiasm must be aroused. If something other than an accepted scripted play is considered there will be clear reasons for this. To attempt an opera will require voices capable of singing the parts and the co-operation of the Music Department; a performance involving much dancing will probably be inspired by some special interest in the school.

An increasingly common form of performance is a play devised, researched and written by the school, probably by pupils and teachers in collaboration. This enables a script to be constructed to suit the talents and skills of the performers, to employ a cast of whatever size is convenient, to exploit the school's

facilities to the full and, in particular, to involve a much larger
'team' in the whole activity. For example, the first idea might be
an historical event or period in some foreign country; the research
required to explore and develop the idea and provide the necessary background can involve the History, Geography, Language,
Art and Music departments and can be used to enliven lessons in
these subjects in many parts of the school. The writing of the text
can be the work of many hands in collaboration and as rehearsals
proceed, re-writing is possible to build a more coherent whole. In
this way a very large number of people can be involved in the
performance with obvious benefits, but the exclusive use of this
method, so that a scripted play is never attempted, would have
limitations. Such a play may involve a large cast; if it does there is
the danger, already noted, that the parts become small with consequent reduction in involvement and challenge for the actor.
Further, the events presented will inevitably be considered by the
pupils in the light of their own necessarily limited experience,
while a scripted play challenges them to consider situations and
characters in the context of a wider experience than their own.
In preparation, rehearsal and later, efforts must be made to keep
the pupils aware of other possible views. From the actors' point
of view, the characters in such plays can easily become caricatures,
or at best, rather 'flat' – it takes a great writer to create rounded
characters – and there is less 'meat' and challenge to the actor. A
valuable part of such a production is often discussion after each
performance, between the audience and the participants, where
the basic ideas and the performance are discussed. Such a discussion needs skilful Chairmanship, but the actors may, in this
way, discover something of their success in putting their ideas
across, and all those involved may be led to consider their work
from a different viewpoint and in the light of the comments, ideas
and suggestions put forward by the audience.

In rehearsals a careful balance must be kept to produce an
effectively staged performance without stifling the creativity of
the actors. The producer must be responsible for the main
groupings, movements, climaxes and pace of the performance,
and the overall interpretation, but wherever possible he will make
the cast themselves work out the details within this framework.
The producer will provide guidelines for the actor to work
within and will behave as a sort of pilot audience to test the
effectiveness and suitability of the actor's ideas, while ensuring

that nothing develops to distort the performance as a whole. The discussions that this approach creates form a most valuable part of the whole business.

To begin with, each actor should be encouraged to read and study the whole play, forgetting, so far as is possible, his own part. Then, with this general view at the back of his mind, he can look at the appearances of the character he is to play, the situations in which the character appears, what he does and says in those situations, always asking himself why the character behaves as he does. This process gradually leads to ideas of the personality which will be the origin of such actions. Thus each actor brings to rehearsal his own interpretation of his part and it is the producer's task to see that the interpretation is valid, plays its appropriate part within the play as a whole, and leads to 'correct' reactions in performance.

In rehearsal, if a line is difficult, or does not 'satisfy' the producer, the approach should be to ask the actor *why* the character says those words. This will probably lead to a digression, with reference to other scenes and to the other characters who will join in the discussion, but in the end will lead to a clearer understanding of the situation, the line and the character. Then the delivery of the line and any accompanying movement or gesture, becomes a matter of effectively communicating to the audience and the other characters. Careful thorough work like this is a slow process and many will feel that the time available for rehearsal does not allow such an approach to be adopted. It is this, more than anything else, that leads to the expediency of demonstration by the producer followed by mimicry by the actor. (It may also be objected that a long discussion with a minor character on the significance of his only line will bore all the other actors who must wait around meanwhile and thus make the rehearsal as a whole less constructive. The answer to this is sensible organization so that the minor character is worked with on his own.) Rehearsal time is always limited and it may not always be possible to employ this discussion and exploration method, but in early rehearsals this approach is essential as the producer and cast explore the play and its characters. If a sufficient foundation is laid in this way (and work in drama lessons can help here, of course) many later scenes will inevitably be referred to and will develop more easily when their time comes and the actors will begin to use the same approach themselves, without direct prompting. In this way, not only do the actors achieve a better understanding of the play and its characters but a better performance results as an actor is constantly encouraged to relate all the actions of the character he plays and to weld them into a consistent presentation of that character.

In attempting to portray a character on stage the actor must first look into himself for the qualities and weaknesses of the part. For example, if jealousy is part of the character the actor must find his own streak of jealousy, see how it has affected his own thoughts and actions in order to appreciate the motivation behind the character's actions. In this way he will learn something of himself and may begin to appreciate how our actions result from the interaction of our characters and the situations in which we find ourselves. Thus the studying of a part in depth in this way can lead to a greater self-knowledge, and a more sensitive awareness of others. It may be said that a good producer, or director, by specifying carefully inflexion, gesture and movement can draw from an actor an equally convincing performance. Obviously, a thorough 'drilling' can do something of the sort, and indeed, all actors must learn to 'hold' a performance once they have achieved the appropriate result, but a cast of twenty that have been drilled into twenty different characters by the producer may simply produce twenty copies of the producer playing twenty different parts. An actor who studies and plays a part brings something of himself to the part and it is this which makes the performance live. The twenty mimics will have learnt little beyond the art of imitation.

Some would say that the producer should never demonstrate, but should work, discuss, suggest until the actor himself produces the desired effect; pupils will often ask for a demonstration as they may find this the easiest way of doing what the producer wants. It has already been said that the producer must work to encourage the actor to give expression to the character in his own terms and not as a mimic; but must help him to do so effectively. But we must remember that our actors are untrained and that rehearsal time is limited. Even with unlimited time there are many special skills that are required for successful acting to an audience and although drama lessons may help to build up some of these we must realize that rehearsals are inevitably a continuous training time in movement, speaking and gesture. It is here that some sort of demonstration can be helpful and much more effective than hours of discussion, but again the method and approach is important. Instead of asking the actor to mimic a particular movement or inflection the producer should explain why the desired effect will be communicated in that way. The other actors in the scene can be used as an audience or asked to try it for themselves; a different interpretation can be placed upon the line or movement temporarily and the appropriate expression developed. Thus the actor can begin to learn the techniques he needs and to explore the use of his voice and whole physical body in expressing his character's thoughts and feelings.

It must be clear that a vital ingredient of rehearsals is discipline. The word is used not in the sense of an imposed 'order' but in its true sense and particularly with reference to self-discipline. Both rehearsals and performances make considerable demands on the actors in this way. Once a performance has begun the only people who can control it are the actors; the producer, whatever he may have done before, can do nothing. Controlling the audience is, of course, a very difficult art, but it must be possible for the performance to remain true to itself. This is particularly important in performances where the action has been developed or the play written by the pupils themselves and where there is no 'set text'. To realize that a certain action will easily produce roars of laughter and to appreciate that by overdoing it the balance of a scene or even of the whole play will be upset, and so to 'moderate' his performance accordingly is a worthy challenge for the young actor. If the cast feel that what they are being led towards is a worth-while performance, they will work unstintingly in rehearsal and in performance. But they must feel this and their enjoyment and satisfaction depends to a large extent on attempting to achieve the highest possible standard and to present to the audience a performance that is really worth watching.

Perhaps the greatest value of a production is the team-work involved in it. The play devised, researched, written and produced in the school provides a very striking example of this, where perhaps the whole of the school (or easily the whole of a House, for example) can be involved in one co-operative venture. Teamwork is especially required from actors and helpers working together (in all performances), but the whole enterprise of a production, from the beginning of preparations and rehearsals is a series of interconnected and interlocked activities and the whole stands or falls by the strengths of the different components. Good acting cannot succeed with poor scenery, lighting, effects or costumes; as much care must go into the creation of the desired scenic effect or the clothing of a character as he has taken to study, learn, and rehearse his lines. And what a wealth of creative opportunities all the different crafts of the theatre provide! The satisfaction and pleasure that pupils can get from helping to build a fine set, creating a beautiful sunrise with skilful lighting, making a boy of fifteen look like an old man of seventy, or devising an ingenious piece of machinery to produce a special effect, are equalled by few other activities. In working in these ways and in acting, pupils develop an appreciation of the crafts and skills of the Theatre which sharpens their appreciation and enjoyment of professional productions. Plays in which a major part of the producing, planning, acting and other work, is carried out by pupils, with the necessary advice and encouragement from teachers, provide excellent opportunities for organization and responsibility. And finally, working to a deadline, the Dress Rehearsal, when all must be ready and perfect, provides a valuable stimulus and discipline.

6. The Professional Theatre in and for Schools

Mark Woolgar

THE WHOLE field of Drama in Education, is relatively new – it has grown rapidly in recent years – and it is rather horrifying to realize that the people who write or speak on the subject are comparatively few and that they are wide open to misinterpretation. You've only got to hear a Drama teacher describing his work in what seems to be a very practical way – '. . . in the first lesson I did so and so and in the second lesson I did so and so . . .' – to feel rather worried that some people are going to go away and, with the best of intentions, try to use those methods in a totally different place and with totally different children and that it may well lead to disaster, although I am perfectly aware that if you went to that teacher's school the work would probably appear to succeed. The same consideration applies to professional theatre work in and for schools. However, the experience of, say, Bristol Old Vic's work in schools, may be of real value to another area and my intention is to outline some of the work undertaken by Bristol, as well as other theatres of which I have some knowledge.

I am not going to discuss such groups as Theatre Centre, the British Dance-Drama Theatre and those companies not usually attached to professional theatre buildings, companies which have for many years been undertaking some of the kind of work which is now, with possibly slightly bemusing rapidity, being essayed by certain professional repertory companies. Neither am I going to refer specifically to work with primary schools, mainly because the Bristol Old Vic does not at present undertake any work for them – a number of professional repertory theatres do – although most of the observations I will make about the organization of

this work obviously apply to all of it, whatever age group it may
be concerned with. I am thinking of those repertory companies,
such as Nottingham, Salisbury, Bristol, Exeter and the others,
wherever they may be, who are mainly doing work with children
of eleven years and upward – and, as far as this work is concerned,
it really goes on right up to the twenty-one and twenty-two-year-
olds.

The theatres which do this work organize it in various ways.
The Belgrade Theatre, Coventry, has the most publicized Theatre
in Education team, and one or two other theatres, such as Green-
wich and Sheffield, do have a Theatre in Education Team. The
Coventry model is that of a permanent group of people spending
their whole time in this kind of work, based on the theatre and
using its plant and facilities for some of their activities. The personnel of this team are either actors who have had teaching experience
or they are ex-teachers. The whole operation is well publicized
and, as it is in existence the whole time, it is available to demonstrate its work at conferences and for people to visit it on its home
ground, and for representatives of the organization to go around
and talk about it. The example of the Belgrade Theatre's Team is
possibly misinterpreted by the general public because its work
is largely made possible by the very sizeable grant given by the
Coventry civic authorities to enable the Team to function. Therefore it could not really be imitated elsewhere unless a similar sum
of money was available. Furthermore, as Coventry foots the bill,
it expects the Team to do its work almost entirely in Coventry.
Presumably there is a large area for the Belgrade Theatre outside
Coventry, and one wonders how much benefit this area derives
from the Belgrade's Theatre in Education Team. To give an
example from here, our operative area from Bristol – by operative
I mean we have active contact with schools within this area –
extends as far as Minehead, Swansea, Abergavenny, Cheltenham
and Gloucester, Hereford, Swindon and down to the Wiltshire/
Dorset border. We have nearly 700 educational establishments on
our mailing list, not a single one of these being a primary school.
So a Theatre in Education Team would have to be vast in order to
deal properly with the potential demand of our whole area.
Furthermore, if one examines carefully the apparent Teams at
some other theatres, one finds that they do not exclusively do
schools work. They quite often spend a good deal of time acting
in the theatre's normal presentations. In practice, most of the

repertory theatres doing this work probably have only one or two people engaged to organize it and the actors they have to use are neither a permanent Team nor experienced in the educational field, and are usually appearing in the theatre's shows or have been appearing in a show in the theatre, and will eventually go back into another one. The great publicity Coventry has received may be rather misleading if people think its way of working applies to all theatres which appear to be engaged in similar activities.

What exactly do the various theatres do within this field, however their personnel and administration are arranged? Although the Arts Council issued a report on 'The Professional Theatre and Young People', it was rather an incomplete survey and seemed to be held up in order to coincide with the publication of the Department of Education and Science survey on Drama, so that it was out of date by the time it eventually came into circulation and was not a reliable guide, so I shall describe the various activities in this field in which theatres are involved.

Probably the most publicized undertakings are tours into schools with specially written shows aimed at various age groups. The style of these tours varies according to the predilections of the particular theatre concerned. In Bristol we have so far taken out eight tours into secondary schools in close collaboration with the Education Authority, who ought to take the credit for originally asking us to do so. These are specially written shows, lasting about forty minutes, simply staged on rostra in the school hall, costume amounting to trimmings to basic rehearsal clothes.

The themes treated have varied from the Great Train Robbery and the situation in Cyprus to Advertising (treated as a musical revue) and a rather too flippant look at America, and last time we presented a straightforward story instead of dealing with a 'theme'.

These tours are presented to the fourth year children in secondary schools, largely because that is what the Education Authority wants. In some ways the activity is unsatisfactory. One of the fourth year groups we play to contains over 400 children because it comes from one of the country's largest comprehensive schools, and this is much too large an audience. We have made various experiments in connection with follow-up discussion groups with the children, and these have had their ups and downs. Other theatres do similar tours for different age groups. Whether or not there is a considerable amount of audience participation varies from theatre to theatre. Obviously those theatres which have a Team or several people specially engaged for the work like to pay preliminary visits to the schools before the main visit and then arrange some kind of follow-up afterwards. I think all theatres would say that they attempt some liaison with appropriate teachers beforehand and possibly afterwards.

The depth or value of this aspect of schools work is very difficult to measure. Any professional theatre undertaking it is to some extent at the mercy not only of the facilities of the particular school but also of the availability or otherwise of teachers already undertaking Drama work in the school, and whether the institution is sympathetic or the opposite to the operation, whatever form it may take. Other theatres have taken round extracts from set plays or simply linked extracts from modern plays. The Royal Shakespeare Company's *Theatregoround* is a very definitely 'theatrical' type of offering. The Bristol Old Vic has just finished a tour to sixth forms and further education establishments with N. F. Simpson's *The Form*, Albee's *Zoo Story* and Chekhov's *The Bear*.

I now turn to 'workshop' sessions, involving participation in either the 'Theatre' or 'Drama' way, both in schools and in clubs and Saturday morning sessions. Theatres like Nottingham Playhouse or Coventry Belgrade, which have a good deal of space outside the auditorium, or theatres which have a rehearsal room (or have recently acquired one), such as the renovated Liverpool Playhouse, are in a very good position to carry on what are, in fact, youth theatre activities. Whether these stem from some kind of theatre club or whether they are open to all varies from place to place. On occasion the work may culminate in some kind of actual production. For instance, the Young Stagers at Coventry have done productions of their own partly 'improvised' material in the theatre itself, and at Derby members of the youth group joined the Company in presenting extracts from Mystery Plays in Derby Cathedral. This type of youth theatre work can obviously be undertaken by professional theatre people. However, at Worthing for instance, it is under the aegis of the theatre, but most of the actual work is supervised by teachers sympathetic to the project, not by actual members of the Company. It may be that teachers or other non-professionals are often better fitted for the job than some professional theatre people. After all, as anybody who has ever heard a certain kind of professional talking to an adult drama club will realize, they are not always very realistic about the situation drama-wise outside the professional theatre and will talk airily about, for example, lighting schemes, which are marvellous but just not possible for the group they are talking to.

Most theatres are willing to show parties of young people backstage, which can take quite a time and has to be fitted in between rehearsals. I need about two hours to show a party all round our premises, including both our theatres, and the workshops and wardrobe. It seems to me worthwhile because it does make clear that Theatre is a job, not a particularly glamorous one, and it is a very good opportunity to point out what beginners in the theatre have to do and, indeed, how much they earn. The argument against backstage visits is, of course, that they give away 'the works' and spoil 'the magic'. As far as I am concerned, provided it is done at the right age, the 'magic' is actually increased for most modern children if they know how it is done. They then have some awareness of the complexity of the operation that is going on, unseen by them, when they attend the performance. However, in this connection I did get almost physically attacked by a designer down at the theatre recently. We were arranging a day on which young people were shown a good deal about the mounting of a show, and the particular production used two revolving stages. I wanted to start the day with a completely bare stage and then show how the set was put up and how it worked. The designer was furious because he said this would spoil the performance, as they would know how it was done, and I mentioned his reaction to the young audience in the course of talking to them. I had several letters back from teachers mentioning that those attending had later brought up the point about whether or not the inside information spoiled the experience of the production and, unless teachers were just trying to please me, the general conclusion was that it didn't and that the audience was the more involved for knowing something of the scale of the operation.

The organization and form of days devoted to Theatre in Action Sessions varies considerably from theatre to theatre. For instance, Salisbury Playhouse has done something called an 'Examination Play Day', where some of the Company work publicly in rehearsal terms on a text which is being studied in many of the schools in the district, a play not necessarily in the Company's repertoire, thus involving them in a considerable amount of extra work. The Oxford Playhouse started Schools Days, and we imitated them in Bristol with something called 'Play Plus Days'. These are occasions on which parties arrive by 10.30 a.m. and the form of the morning session is dictated somewhat by the nature of the particular play under scrutiny, but usually those attending learn something about the play, what is involved in staging it, how professionals go about designing a production, what contribution the lighting can make, how rehearsals are conducted and so forth. They may have an opportunity to take part in a scene. For instance, *The Lady's Not for Burning* includes the off-stage noise of a crowd wanting a witch's blood. In the play the crowd never appears but we staged the crowd scene that might have happened if theatre economics allowed. We considered what would be the various reactions of the kinds of people likely to be found in a small medieval township if they did find a witch. We sent people into groups to work on this, aided by members of the Company, and then we did a large crowd scene on far too small a stage and saw how this worked out, and were able to make certain points about characterization, 'improvised' versus directed scenes, grouping and so forth. It may have been a bit ragged but I think it did make several points very clearly, perhaps the more so for not being slickly rehearsed.

In the afternoon those attending see a complete performance of the play which they have learned something about in the morning and which is, in fact, the play we are presenting in the evenings. If there is time afterwards they may look round the stage or have conversations with members of the cast and production team, whom they have already become familiar with during the morning session. The cost is 5s. a head for the 'Day'. Other theatres do similar things, though I don't think very many do whole days in the theatre actually related to the current production, except sometimes in connection with a Shakespeare play or something 'classical'. I think more of this should be done and, provided one chooses the date carefully, it can take place on a day when rehearsals are not scheduled, so the routine work of the theatre does not suffer.

Courses for teachers have probably been undertaken less often, though a Theatre in Education team should be well fitted to run them, and people who are undertaking schools work with companies are likely to be asked to go and take part in courses for teachers organized by others. Exhibitions can be sent out. We have thirteen double-sided display boards, as well as boxes to contain set models and we usually have two exhibitions out on free loan and probably other additional material in various schools on the schools' own display boards. One is frequently asked to go and give talks of various kinds, formal and informal, or to judge drama competitions, verse speaking competitions and kindred events. All of this seems worth doing, provided one always bears in mind the facilities which the group one is visiting have to work with. Other help Companies can give to youth organizations can be of a very practical nature, in terms of the loan of costumes and other equipment at special rates, free gifts of still useful equipment which the theatre no longer requires, and general technical advice.

Some people say that once a professional theatre starts any work with schools it can easily tread on the preserves of some other theatre and there is a limit to the amount of work schools will respond to: my experience has not borne this out. While I was in a secondary modern school in Wiltshire talking to some of the older children about production, I learned that during the previous term the General Manager of the Salisbury Playhouse had talked about theatre management to the fifth year, and in the coming term they hoped to get somebody, preferably from another theatre, to talk about design.

The same school had had two trips to Stratford and regularly visits the Salisbury Playhouse and our two Bristol theatres, sometimes for 'Play Plus Days'. That degree of interest is not untypical of many of the 160 schools I have visited in the last two years. I know of a school in Cardiff which was in the habit of sending parties to the Schools Days at the Oxford Playhouse, which is quite a considerable distance; when we began 'Play Plus Days' they started to come to us, and now they use both Oxford and Bristol. On one of our tours to fourth year children in Bristol secondary schools, one school asked whether we could come on another day within the fortnight in which we were touring because they were going to Oxford for a Schools Day. Although there are schools where nothing at all happens in this direction, there are many, often not particularly near a theatre, where the demand is enthusiastic and voracious.

In visiting the schools in our area or seeing the activities of various youth theatre groups, one is given many vivid reminders

D

of the considerable body of theatrical skills to be found amongst young people, showing themselves in performances of many different kinds. I see this as a healthy illustration of this dictum from the Department of Education and Science Survey:

> There must be two objectives to any policy for Drama in a school. One is to provide opportunities for the personal development of the young people, the other is to direct them towards an appreciation of Drama and the Theatre Arts. These objectives are not exclusive. The one, in fact, should lead towards the other.

I happen to agree with that, but I know that not all Drama teachers do; I recall the teacher at a Drama conference in London who told me, 'I never take the children to the theatre. It's not my job as a Drama teacher. In fact, I hardly ever go to the theatre myself.' I understand him, I respect his principles, but I agree with the statement in the Report. As a Theatre worker, I must define what I mean by the difference, in educational terms, between Drama and Theatre.

Drama in the educational sense, as I imagine it is being practised by Drama teachers, is child-centred, which Theatre is not. It is child-centred because, whatever form it takes, it is basically concerned with the development of the children's imagination, sensitivity, all the other usual words, but the essential point is that it is basically concerned with the children. To my mind, that immediately sets it apart from any activity you can call Theatre, because when children who have been doing drama work in a school engage in something which is more clearly defined as Theatre, they are almost certainly working towards something which is shaped and polished, is in some way 'artistic', is almost certainly, but not necessarily, going to be presented to an audience and is, in any case, rather more self-conscious and 'presented' than pure Drama work. All that applies to theatrical performances wherever they take place, whether conventionally on a proscenium stage or in the form of an 'improvisation' which has been reworked many times to arrive at a final form. It does not suggest something essentially child-centred, as the work in Drama lessons should be, if properly designed. I would have thought this indicates a basic and recognizable difference between Theatre and Drama in an educational context.

This leads me to wonder whether professional theatre people

have any particular place in the Drama work in schools, if it is child-centred and has to do with the development of children. I am not at all convinced that their training and preoccupations particularly fit them for involvement in this work. Even Theatre in Education Teams, containing people with teaching experience, must to some extent be inadequate because they don't know the children well enough after even the maximum number of visits they are able to make to any one location, though close co-operation with the right kind of teacher – if such exists – may afford some compensation. It is even possible to envisage an area not very well endowed with Drama teachers where an L.E.A. might think that the activities of a Theatre in Education team were, in themselves, an adequate substitute for more Drama teachers, and I think it would be dangerous if this situation were ever to arise.

So, where exactly does the professional theatre come in? In the first bulletin of the National Council of Theatre for Young People there is this comment: 'The purpose of the work has come in for a great deal of discussion. Theatres say they are trying to fill a gap in education. If so, they must identify the nature of the gap.' The D.E.S. Survey states:

> The growing interest of the professional theatre in education is of the greatest significance. Enthusiasm must now be tempered with policy. The theatre must seek out the ways in which it can make its particular contribution to educational practice and the schools must decide upon the nature of the help they want from professional actors and producers. ... The only basis for a permanent arrange-ment can be mutual agreement on what trained theatre people can do for schools that the schools cannot do for themselves. Far more discussion on this crucial issue is necessary than seems hitherto to have taken place. If the answer is that more time and so more money are needed, one can only say that the work of the theatre will have to be tailored to the amount that is available. Projects should not be started that cannot be adequately carried through.

The nature of 'the gap' must be defined. It seems that it has got to be a definite gap, something the schools cannot fill for them-selves, and that possible methods of filling it must then be sensibly attuned to what is actually, not theoretically, possible at the particular time in the particular circumstances of each indi-vidual theatre undertaking work. Theatre people are theatre people, not educationists. The very fact that they are theatre people may actually make them a liability in the schools.

It may be that a Theatre in Education Team of the Coventry kind, a mixture of teachers and actors working from a theatre, is the ultimate perfection, but I say *ultimate* perfection because, in the forms in which it can exist at the moment, it can only do a certain scraping of the surface. In any case, if it is connected to a theatre its effectiveness will probably be related to the policy of that particular theatre in other directions besides the Theatre in Education Team. It might be that a Theatre in Education Team unattached to a theatre, but financed perhaps by an education authority in a particular area, would be an interesting innovation, provided it worked in co-operation with such drama teachers as already existed. I believe there are people who are thinking along these lines and it would be interesting to see what this half-way house between a theatre-based group and an ordinary school drama teacher might produce.

What exactly is the gap we can fill now and how should we start to fill it? The size of the generalized demand made upon us is ridiculous in terms of constructive work. The one-act play tour we took out, aimed only at sixth forms, was asked for by so many places that we could have toured for eight weeks. We had to refuse many schools and we tried to do this only where the school was reasonably near a theatre. It became clear that in this work one can either make an arguably ineffective foray over a large field or try to be really effective in a few schools.

I do not wish to be dogmatic about the type of activity we should engage in, but I should have thought that days when children come to the theatre and are really told about how the theatre works and then see a play are useful, as are exhibitions, talks and showing children round the premises, and that tours into educational establishments are worth-while, provided they are planned carefully in co-operation with the institutions they are to visit. In this connection it may seem surprising that we took what might be regarded as an unsuitable play, *Zoo Story*, on tour to sixth formers. In fact, before we chose that programme we circulated to all the schools on our relevant mailing list a schedule of plays we could tour, and asked them to tell us which plays they would definitely like and which plays they would certainly not accept, and to leave the others unclassified. *Zoo Story* came easily top of the list of desirable plays, and created considerable interest in the schools in which it was performed. The kind of activities I have mentioned do, I think, fill a gap which the schools could not fill for themselves and can, in large part, be successfully undertaken by theatre people who have no particular experience in education.

I am under no illusion that these activities necessarily build 'Tomorrow's Audience', nor do I think that this is a vital consideration. I am not one of those people who feels the theatre must sell out to youth: we have a sufficient youth cult as it is. Young people are not the only patrons of the theatre and they won't be young for ever. But I do think it is very important indeed that a large number of young people should know about theatre, should have an introduction to it. They should know that it is a normal activity open to all and that it is available to them almost as a right. They are going to be taxpayers and ratepayers and a small amount of their taxes and rates will keep the professional theatres going: they are in the widest possible sense the patrons of the modern theatre, as they are of such places as museums and art galleries. It must be remembered that during and after the last war many theatre buildings – often not housing 'Legitimate' Theatre – were demolished, and there were as yet very few subsidized theatres; when the parents of the children in the schools today were teenagers, theatrical facilities were very limited. One has only to talk to children in many of the comprehensive schools in our area to find that theatre simply does not feature in their parents' lives, and the older members of their families may even be mildly amused that these children go to the theatre, initially in parties arranged by schools. There is, therefore, a considerable social barrier between the theatre and much of the public, created by historical accident and the fact that subsidy for the theatre came later than it ought to have done in an ideal world, so that the theatres' programmes and attitude to the public changed rather later than they should have done. I do not mind in the least if the young people to whom we are giving a glimpse of theatre via our liaison with schools don't all come to the theatre in later life. What I would like to feel is that if, in twenty years' time in a conversation at the pub, somebody was to say, 'I see there's a row about whether they should go on giving this grant to the theatre,' there would be more people capable of considering the matter without the total ignorance and prejudice likely to exist today because so many of today's parents know nothing about theatre. If, when they are older, today's young people choose to spend their leisure time elsewhere than in the theatre, as many of them will, that doesn't particularly matter, but the climate in which theatres can work is made just as much by the people who don't go to the theatre as by the people who do; this is important for an art which is alive only while it is being practised. The breaking down of the social barrier is something which matters; that is not the same thing as cynically justifying schools activities as simply building 'Tomorrow's Audience'.

There are weaknesses in any work for schools which theatres may undertake, especially since most theatres do not have special Theatre in Education Teams. I suspect that in a number of theatres the work is organized by a person with little understanding of the educational scene, who may well take less trouble than he should to remedy this deficiency, merely sitting in his office and sending out lots of circulars. There is absolutely no substitute for going out and about: school teachers, like almost everybody else, receive far too much gratuitous paper, and it is all too easy to write to the wrong person; by the time one reaches the right person it is too late.

Then there are weaknesses brought about by the financial instability of many of the schemes undertaken. This is very important because subsidy is meant to enable theatres to plan ahead, but the subsidies are still not guaranteed very far in advance and the amount available for schools work is slender. At Bristol we have received a grant from the Arts Council, specifically for schools work, only in the financial year just finishing, and it is £1,000, and next year it will be reduced to £750. I am not employed entirely to do schools work, but a portion of that money goes into my salary (though I actually earn less now than when I gave up teaching after three years). That doesn't leave a great deal over. Furthermore, unless one is able to plan a long way ahead one is not in a very good position to treat with education authorities for a share of their money, and one is lucky if one gets any under the present circumstances. So the work is usually done on a pretty shaky financial basis.

The work is often badly organized because the career structure in the theatre is still largely geared to 'moving on'; though teachers also move on, there is a much greater sense of continuity of administration in schools. In practical terms this means that an educationist may deal with three different people at a particular theatre in as many years, no one of them staying long enough to know the situation in the area thoroughly. I feel that this constant change is more likely to result in inefficiency than stimulating variety.

I have suggested that theatre people can be a distinct liability, even if technically operating within their own field. It is not just that they may not take into account the particular situation of the people to whom they are talking, but they are often surprisingly bad speakers. The idea of getting the children in a theatre and telling them how the production works and asking the designer and director and so forth to come on can be a disaster. They cannot be heard beyond the front rows. This can apply just as much to actors, even if the theatre is blacked out and it is as much like a performance as possible and they know exactly what the questions are. To say, as a number of teachers do, 'Wouldn't it be lovely if all the actors could come to school,' might be to court a terrible 'flop'.

Then there are the dangers of lip service from the top directors of the theatres which do some of this work as part of their activities. I am not at all sure they are all as interested as they say they are when they get up on public occasions, and this can have considerable bearing on the type of people likely to be appointed by the director to look after schools work, and on the relationship between those involved in schools work and the rest of the Company.

The work that we may undertake in schools is often nullified by the attitude existing in the school: just before the performance is about to begin up jumps Miss X and bellows at Maude to shut up, or perhaps a play like *Zoo Story* offends somebody, and the organizer realizes that if he said what he ought to say to the Headmaster, who is now worried, he will completely queer the pitch for the single member of staff who is an ally.

Finally, many teachers are unwilling to criticize constructively the work undertaken. This is very regrettable, especially when somebody with little experience of schools is running the work at the theatre. It may seem patronizing, but I am saddened by the almost pathetically grateful letters I get from teachers saying how wonderful it all is – particularly after a 'Play Plus Day' which I know was inadequate and shallow. This is why it is important to get out and meet the teachers, for then they feel they really can criticize. If they don't, responsibility for the maintenance of standards and for improvement is all thrown back on the theatre, which will not necessarily provide the best inspiration for such progress.

I should like to quote, without further comment, the letter which has given me most pleasure recently, and I hope the reader will see why I found it heartening. The letter is from a teacher, and perhaps the teacher is too effusive. The boy quoted in it is the head boy, and we all know that head boys can say what they are expected to say on certain occasions, though that seems to be cancelled out by other facts that are given. The letter, following the school's visit to a Play Plus Day, came from a mixed county comprehensive secondary school in Swansea: that is also pleasing because it is a long way from Bristol, though I wonder how much the Grand Theatre, Swansea benefits from what we are doing. Here it is:

> The general opinion of the pupils who attended was summed up by the Head Boy who remarked, 'One of the most fantastic days of my life. I had no idea Theatre could be so exciting.' Most of my pupils come from culturally deprived homes. Indeed, it might interest you to know that of the 38 pupils who attended only two had been inside a professional theatre before. We have a flourishing theatre club at school and pupils pay in small weekly amounts to defray the expenses of forthcoming theatre visits. After our visit to the Old Vic the queue next day reached the end of a long corridor, all wanting to pay towards the next trip. I do hope you will be able to accommodate us as often as possible. I would like to thank all the Company for the magnificent work they are doing.

Remember, only two had been to the professional theatre before. The play they saw, believe it or not, was Otway's *Venice Preserved*.

PART TWO

The second part contains the reports of the various discussion groups. Each group discussed the place of drama in education as a whole and then went on to develop one particular theme more fully. In the reports the division between the general and particular discussions is not always rigidly adhered to; some of the reports are gnomic in places; there are contradictions between reports; and there is a great variety of views.

It was hoped, at one stage, to edit the reports for easier reading. However, in the event, it was felt that variety of presentation and method would not only make this difficult but substantial editing might seriously distort the different views expressed and emphases implied.

It is suggested that these reports should be read in conjunction with the appropriate discussion papers to be found in Appendix II.

Reports from Discussion Groups

1. *Meaning and purpose of Drama in Classroom*

(a) To give information and the responsibility to take a role where confrontation comes with a situation, problem, attitude; and by experiencing these the children satisfy a need at that time.

(b) So: improvisation and plays should be structured or selected to satisfy the present personal needs.

(c) Allow elaboration from personal experience of children. Needs for all groups/classes are different. It is better to satisfy personal needs by using children's experience.

(d) Teacher notices personal needs of individual child; be aware of reactions; who is isolated, thinking, feeling, so teacher can assess feedback for each individual child; so bring social capacity, imaginative capacity and personal needs into classroom for satisfaction and fulfilment by playreading and improvisation.

(e) This will bring more into the child's experience than can be brought by simply *discussion* or *talk*. Drama will bring more surprise, more feeling, awareness of others' attitudes and needs – a general widening of experience and personal development.

(f) There must be encouragement of the element to agree on pretence.

(g) Teacher must bring adult experience in pre-digested form, which the children can absorb, *at that time* for those *particular* needs.

(h) To satisfy these needs, *know* the present situation in the school and in the classroom/group. Since the end of drama work is unknown, it can lead to a variety of confrontations, new attitudes, and can satisfy a variety of group needs. Valuable in developing social and imaginative capacities. Can satisfy group/school/area/ individuals/syllabus. It will teach a child to take attitudes and responsibilities to problems and situations both in his own sphere and in those of other people.

(*i*) Teacher must watch reactions – who wants to act, to distract, to think, to feel, to resolve a need, resolve personal problem.

2. *School Play*

Should be a polished performance within the rules of the Theatre. Extract and discuss ideas in the play – watch reactions and cast finally from these reactions.

3. All drama in school must be related to: feedback, ideas, feelings and emotional experience, excitement. So teacher should have final control over *content*.

4. So: drama in school will be different in different areas. Content should be related to social factors, home and experience factors. So variety of feedback in variety of areas – different feedback, different conflicts and excitements, different confrontations must be given to children in different areas.

5. *Essential teacher has knowledge of theatre*

This means knowing how to structure a play or improvisation: how to use stillness or silence; limitations and orbit of room; lights, colour, costume, grouping (physical and emotional); oral and mental feedback to improve and elaborate situation, movement – but *avoid* 'elocution'.

So theatre technique must be in blood of teacher.

So teacher can develop and express through the group and the acting a confrontation set in the total orbit of the room and within the children's mental and social needs.

So teacher can give the *correct drives* and lead the children into imaginative areas that *are right* for the situation at that time. But *teacher must know* the area, the school tone, the individuals.

6. *Release of new energies*

The drama and theatre techniques will release new energies and develop new skills, and direct these into art, design, music, wardrobe, ceramics, engineering, lighting, administration and organizing, printing, original verse and plays leading to exhibitions and projects.

Drama is a release of physical and mental energies. Teacher must direct and control these.

New questions, new attitudes can be expressed in verse, etc. So integration of subjects can be encouraged.

But the teacher must always be aware of individual needs, aware of social attitudes around the children outside and inside the school. So it is a two-way problem: the teacher guides, directs and selects material while children reveal problems, attitudes, needs and experience to be satisfied. So this leads to a *continual growth* of child's mind and personality, i.e. *communication* and *development*: communication through a wide variety of experiences and skills.

DISCUSSION GROUP NO. 1(b)
LEADER: MISS W. HICKSON

GENERAL DISCUSSION

The discussion opened with general comments on the performance seen on the previous evening of *Guns*.[1] The following points were raised.

1. Were we worried by the fact that the cast had pushed the problems of the hypocrisy of the Adult world, which was the underlying theme of their improvisation, on to America and not faced it within their own environment?

2. *Presentation*
   (*a*) Had they got the necessary technique to bring this type of work to performance level?
   (*b*) If the teacher had come into the production at a late stage and served as a producer and improved the technical details, would it have removed the spontaneity and bite from their performance?
   (*c*) By taking an active part, would not the teacher have been able to encourage the less forceful characters (e.g. the girls) to contribute more to the improvisation?

Conclusion. After discussion it was agreed that the aim of this work was that it was a process of maturing and casting off. The fact that these young people had been completely self-sufficient, and had felt in no need of the teachers' support surely spoke for its purpose and value. This is success and what education is about.

The meeting then moved on to discussing the ways into text from Improvisation. The improvisation leading into the Gettysburg Address[2] seen during the Session with the Students was

[1] See Appendix IV.
[2] See John Hodgson: Improvisation and Literature, pp. 37–9.

mulled over. How could the texture and deep meaning of the language be retained, and not become trivial as in the Student improvisation. Was it justifiable to present material which was anyway historically untrue? Surely there was a need to examine the language sympathetically, relate it to the period and not send it up? (It would be possible to send up even a Shakespeare Sonnet!) Was it done to remove the mystic from the Gettysburg Address? If so, it failed and just made it pointless and cheap.

TEACHER TRAINING

The meeting then discussed, leading on from the thoughts about improvisation, whether students in training were given sufficient understanding of the fact that certain improvisation exercises were at the students' own level and for their own growth and development. Was it made plain to them that some of these exercises were not necessarily the right approach for children?

Concern was expressed by the group that Students did not always understand this – and should be made much more aware of it by their tutors – and given a deeper understanding of how to use this material.

How is it possible to stimulate imagination and sensitive thinking and use of material with Students who are just not up to it? Is it possible to teach this intuitive thinking, which tells a Student what to do in any situation in a Drama lesson, when to take an active role and participate in the improvisation, when to withdraw completely and when and how to guide it? Is it just something which comes with experience – or can it be taught? (No conclusion was reached!)

Could more training be given in Group dynamics – and in challenging both teachers and Students to examine deeply their role as teachers? Is sufficient time being given to Students to discuss why they failed or succeeded in the classroom and why? A Student member of the group said that this was dependent on the relationship between the individual student and her tutor.

The School Play was then discussed. It was felt that a standard should be set, so that the children could aim for excellence, and feel justly proud of their achievement. A tradition of high artistic standard could be built up in a School over the years, with other departments (Music, Art, Woodwork, Needlework) joining together to make a successful production. Why do children and teachers need this love and admiration that this success brings? Is it because they lack it from other sources?

THE PLACE OF THE SPECIALIST TEACHER OF DRAMA WAS DISCUSSED

It was felt that a valuable contribution could be made by a Specialist Drama Teacher – provided that Drama did not become a sacred subject only 'done' at set times by the Drama Specialist, but that all members of staff used it in the classroom situation as a teaching tool in its deepest sense.

SUMMARY OF GROUP DISCUSSION. GROUP 1(b)

(The group was pleased to welcome Gavin Bolton for this session) The discussion during the time allowed covered a great deal of ground which included the most valuable interchanging of ideas and examples of the use of drama by members of the group in a variety of situations.

For the purposes of this summary it will be convenient to say at the outset that the discussion concerned itself with the following main areas:

(i)   Drama – the medium, its uses and functions.
(ii)   Relating the medium to children at various stages in their development – particularly adolescence.
(iii) The establishing of relationships with a class and finding ways in with drama.
(iv)   The teacher's role in relation to a group's efforts in drama – how much criticism, interruptions, etc.
(v)   The training of student teachers in the light of all this.

(i) Drama is able to deal with experience and bring it to life – hence the definition in Dorothy Heathcote's paper:

Persons   Now   Conflict

As one member of the group put it, as a teacher of English, he feels he is dealing with 'man alive in his total environment'.

Drama can increase a child's awareness of self and others, this is fairly certain, but how does the teacher help this awareness to develop?

What kind of material does one use?

These are the constant questions in the teacher's mind, who

may be well aware of the nature of the medium, its effect and advantages, but what does he do when confronted with the class of thirty, perhaps for the first time?

The basic consideration must always be the relationship between teacher and group of children: the teacher must know his own role within a group and allow children to gain his confidence.

The group was in constant agreement about these basic matters as they had been so aptly put before them by Dorothy Heathcote on the previous Tuesday and summarized so well in her own conference paper.[1]

(ii) Ways in which drama will obviously vary. It sounds commonplace, but it is true to say, it all depends on the group of children concerned at any given time. Material that 'worked' with a group one year, will not necessarily be successful with a comparable group the next year. One needs constantly to take soundings of a group at the outset. The children will usually give pointers as to what they would like to do, what kind of area they want to explore. One group member here raised the question: Is there not a danger that we are catering for the children's wants rather than their needs, allowing them self-indulgence?

This is to be guarded against. The teacher must be aware of the capabilities of a group and therefore of their needs, be it in terms of language demands, social or emotional needs or whatever.

It was at this point that Gavin Bolton gave a fine example from his experience of a group working on their wants and the teacher structuring the situation according to their needs:

The group: bright grammar school children – mixed 12–13 years.

Their wants: girls a mannequin parade, boys robbers.

Girls go off and prepare for parade etc.

Boys together with teacher plan a robbery.

Why not rob the girls, their furs, handbags, etc.

So far so good!

At this point the teacher was able to build into the situation something that would cater for the needs of these particular children. They were very able with words and here was something to develop. Each boy was told to get into conversation with one of the girls and to find out as much information as possible (which would be needed for the robbery) about the mannequin parade,

[1] See Appendix II.

without letting the girl know that he was doing so. (Situations in cafés, bus-stops, trains, etc. here were evolved by children.) Thus a particular moment had been created which put demands linguistically upon the children. It would be important to allow them still to have the ultimate 'kick' from their wants, and to have their parade and robbery.

(iii) It was agreed that communication between teacher and group can be at its most difficult at the adolescent stage in development. It is almost impossible to suggest material to use, say in a 'mixed middle-school' class. However helpful it is to swop accounts of classroom experiences in drama with one's colleagues (and the group was agreed on the vital importance of such exchanges amongst teachers) the choice of material for and ways in to a group will finally depend upon that group with that particular teacher. One needs patience with oneself as a teacher, in developing gradually the intricate relationships required in the teaching situation.

Here, a member of the group raised the problem of quicker and slower children within a class. How does one 'get through' to the slower ones and supply opportunity for self-expression.

The teacher must be able to structure a situation whereby the brighter or quicker ones are constricted: example given might be a space ship losing contact with earth – the quicker children being in the ship – thus the slower ones have to cope with a situation themselves. But whatever the problem, it demands tremendous awareness on the teacher's part and a readiness to give a lot of time to thinking about any given class and its needs. At the same time the teacher must be prepared to respect the quiet, slower pupil, who might not take immediate part in dramatic activity, but who nevertheless might make valuable contributions in other ways.

(iv) How often and how much should the teacher structure children's work and apply criticism at various levels?

The basic requirement is that the work should relate to something. A group must discover an area to work on. The teacher can take a minor role and thus be enabled to influence the course of the situation *from within*. In this way the teacher is often able to help children to move on and out of a groove they might have got into.

(v) This relates immediately to the problem of training teachers in the use of drama as an effective tool in teaching. How is it possible to help a teacher (student or in-service) to know these moments to come in on what a group is doing, to make the best use of what the children offer?

Gavin Bolton: We need to develop a basic sensitivity to classes and to individuals. Analyse what is happening in the medium (as observer); Ask oneself always: (*a*) What is lacking here? (*b*) Why is this not working and developing? (*c*) What element is missing? (*d*) How can I make it real and living for the children?

Most commonly in such work there is a lack of the particular within a broad generalization. The teacher needs to develop an ability to build in motivation, conflict, immediacy, into the children's situation.

Here again Gavin Bolton gave a lucid and helpful description of an example of this process: Group of young children working on *The Plague*. They were generalizing, 'dying all over the place'. 'They were thrilled with it and it was horrible!' The teacher builds in an element of surprise: declaration that all cats and dogs must be killed.

This allays the general death theme and particularizes the feelings of people about their favourite pet animals. Immediately, they have another, more demanding situation to deal with, a microcosm within the whole.

Finally, the group was agreed on the duality of the teacher's role in work of this nature. When children are engaged in dramatic activity, making a 'nowness' of particular events, the teacher must be able (i) to be with the children imaginatively (ii) to stand outside and apart from them, observing.

The constant recognition of one's mistakes is valuable and matters a great deal in the development of this rather intricate, sensitive approach to children and their work. There are certainly no quick and easy answers, but there are firm guide lines being mapped out for student and in-service teachers alike, by people who have proved themselves and their ideas in work with children.

DISCUSSION GROUP NO. 2
LEADER: G. RAWLINS

MOVEMENT AND DRAMA

Summary of Important Points made on Wednesday's Seminar

1. The secondary curriculum is killing the concept of what drama ought to be – all other subjects as well! Cutting off artificially by periods on timetable when interest is going (team teaching, flexible timetable, breath of spring of middle schools).
2. Aims of drama teaching:
(i) Development of child – personality, confidence (and confidence not only in himself but in being accepted in a group) – experiments with life in a 'safe' world.
(ii) Aware of all his senses.
(iii) Speech flexibility, clarity of thought, listening concentration.
3. Concern for standards of many professional theatre groups visiting schools – importance of teachers' liaison in their visits – if possible, teachers working with actor/teachers in some local drama centre.
4. That *all* students in colleges of education should be made *dramatically aware* (a basic drama course for all) and that when teaching, opportunities should exist for them keeping in touch with dramatic developments (teachers' centres, in-service training, regular social get-togethers).
5. Some kind of 'drama space' should be available in all schools, to establish the priority of the subject. A drama 'specialist' should be appointed in all middle and secondary schools not to teach drama full-time but to assist other teachers in the school to help them gain confidence in this sort of work and to integrate the work generally.

Points from Thursday morning's Seminar on Movement with Mrs Sherborne[1]

1. Through movement a child gains *awareness* of self, others, and the ground. For example, facial awareness can be developed by such methods as follows:
(i) Making faces at partner, expand face, contract face, etc.

[1] This should be read in conjunction with Veronica Sherborne's paper on Movement for Drama, pp. 63–72.

(ii) Feeling faces.
(iii) Eyes following a track.
(iv) Staring at partner's eyes while moving away or closer.
(v) Looking closely at colour of eyes.
(vi) Darting eyes.
2. General structure of a lesson.
   Contrast in movement must be built into the lesson (i.e. force/
gentleness) but lessons should be intuitive.
Main movement qualities:
(i) Energy – from forceful to very gentle.
(ii) Flow – bound flow (controlled movement) or free flow (as
      in waltz or tennis service).
(iii) Time – from fast to very slow to stillness.
(iv) Space – confined space, open space, straight – winding
      pathways, etc.
Lesson should offer experiences of different qualities of movement.
Use free flow to start a lesson as this is uninhibiting, and then use
bound flow later on. Likewise, in general, strong movement first,
delicate movement later.
3. *Other Points*
(i) Initial embarrassment – teacher can help to overcome this by
      moving herself, taking a partner. Concrete suggestions for
      movement are needed – i.e. how can you move on the earth?
      slither, crawl, etc.
(ii) Aggression – This is worked out in movement lesson.
      Advisable not to have pairs from opposite sexes at first for such
      exercises.
(iii) Relaxation – successful method consists in lying backwards
      over partner on all fours, head hanging loose.
(iv) Dress – Trousers or tights, bare feet.
(v) Music – Used with beginners mostly, but it can dictate too
      much and prevent extension. Singing and movement together
      is good.
(vi) Size of class and classroom – 30 is too big, but when this is
      unavoidable in school some work can be done with half class
      sitting down, the other half working. It is important to break
      class into small, flexible groups. One can cope in a classroom
      but more space is obviously better.
(vii) Movement training – Teachers should attend movement
      sessions before they teach. Martha Graham system gives
      confidence, but lacks feeling, is forceful and very controlled –

not suitable for children. Merce Cunningham techniques not suitable for children.

DISCUSSION GROUP NO. 4
LEADER: M. WOOLGAR

THE PROFESSIONAL THEATRE IN AND FOR SCHOOLS

Summary of discussions in discussion group which opted to discuss 'The Professional Theatre in and for Schools' – No attempt has been made to differentiate which period of discussion contained which thoughts! – Also it should be pointed out that a majority of those in the group were professionally concerned with the subject they had opted to discuss, which may explain the limits and limitations of the discussion!

First, it was felt important that we should define what was meant by Drama in Education (i.e. improvisation, etc., rather than professional companies going into schools).

A number of suggestions were made: there was something in it for every child; it stimulated the imagination and developed the spirit; it was something inherent in every child that needed bringing out. No decision was finally reached on this topic but it led to discussion on:

The improbability of attempting to define Drama. There could be considerable diversity of Drama going on in school and all of it might well be valuable, be it scripted play or improvisation. Individual teachers might have difficulty in developing work in some ways, so each must be left to find his own way of working through Drama. This led to a discussion on –

The need to define the aim of Drama. Perhaps it was not sufficient to say that all ways were satisfactory, since it was essential to know when Drama work was, educationally speaking, at its best. It was essential that you should be clear on the aims of doing Drama, so that you knew the exact purpose of what you were doing at any particular time.

A Drama student talked of the need to build up his own philosophy towards Drama. He found that on teaching practice he did work that often connected with other subjects and other teachers. He felt that he should present the children with a situation and let them feel something from it – and it seemed reasonable to suppose that the aim of the lesson should not necessarily be present before the actual lesson began. This was dependent on how well the teacher knew the children and brought us on to –

Teacher/Pupil relations. How important it was to know the children you taught. If dealing with a new group of children it was essential to take soundings before deciding where to begin. You needed to know how to handle the children and when to ask the right questions – timing was very important. It was suggested that to start with Movement might establish confidence but not every teacher would feel competent to use this.

We then moved on to consider how this pupil/teacher relationship, once established, would be affected by the coming in to the school of a Theatre in Education team. The general feeling was that it was unsatisfactory for any Professional Theatre Groups to go into schools and give Drama lessons. When any sort of professional group took such lessons they must not be in isolation but must be part of a bigger theme. It was felt that when the children were used it was very important that there should be liaison with the teacher and that the teacher should be trusted to choose the right children to be used.

This led on to discussion of the importance of the Professional Theatre in schools, whether a Theatre in Education group attached to a theatre or a professional group drawn from the theatre 'proper'. Here a number of points were made:

(*a*) A good deal of stress was laid on liaison with teachers – and even suggestion that teachers should be involved in the programme. Certainly a pre-visit talk with the teacher was important, as was follow up with the children.

(*b*) Such visits could be very useful to Liberal Studies Departments for instance, by presenting social problems, so tying the theatre to other areas of studies and suggesting a follow-up in several subjects, e.g. History.

(*c*) In Educational Drama in Schools there was not enough progression and the Theatre in Education could help the lively teacher to the progression that was necessary.

(*d*) The professional actor going into the school was most important to provide a stimulus for teacher and children.

(*e*) The professionals made the point that they wished the teachers in secondary schools were not so anxious for programmes to be geared to external examinations.

(*f*) The importance of having actor/teachers.

(*g*) If using purely professional actors there is tie-up, as children can go to see them on stage.

We then considered the different types of professional theatre in schools –

(i) The new types of theatres which tend to be community theatres and to have a Theatre in Education team attached to them.

(ii) The old type of theatres – where schools work is done through a theatre/school organizer, using professional actors, and where the hazards and tensions in the organization of school/theatre liaison are much greater.

The point was made that, as well as bringing the theatre to the schools, the teachers should take the children to the theatre.

Another point on the subject of Drama – that it must lead children towards knowing what various forms of art are and this should help eventually in giving them standards. A speaker then said that Drama was an art form since young children, when doing Drama, are using the elements of theatre (e.g. conflict) but because it was being used, it didn't mean that your main study was an art form.

A number of problems more particularly concerned with the 'professional' side of things were aired: actors sometimes not keen; difficulties in theatres where the chief director is not really committed to the work; project work based on the plays in the theatre's repertoire; Schools Tours using regional material for specially written documentaries; can a Theatre in Education group exist completely separate from a theatre? difficulties facing actor/teachers who, by the theatre itself, may be regarded as second class actors and used only unwillingly for plays in the theatre. What is the status of the actor/teacher in relation to the main company; use of design department from the ordinary theatre; Arts Council grants and the hope that eventually theatres would get more money for educational work from L.E.A.s; the ethics of various schemes of remuneration for actors taking part in 'educational 'work; what do the teachers want from professional companies; difficulty of getting really good actors to do this work in schools; necessity of keeping up standards; using individual professionals in schools, rehearsing some dramatic activity alongside young people (e.g. opera at Cranleigh).

DISCUSSION GROUP NO. 5/12
LEADER: W. BOSENCE

CHILDREN'S GAMES

This group began by reiterating the vital importance of Dorothy Heathcote's phrase 'Laughter kills'.

Children in play have their own strictly worked out and adhered to rules. They show so much energy – why then does this disappear in school? It need not do so if the right attitude and sympathetic approach is adopted by the teacher or play leader. Even such games as football are not merely straight-forward games but an acting out of what the players would like to be, e.g. George Best. We do not know exactly when play starts but it is certainly very early, e.g. the three-year-old with a matchbox along a wall pretending – perhaps unconsciously – that it is a cat. There are a very great many different kinds of play – free, separate, uncertain, unregulated, mimicry, competitive games, vertigo games and games of chance. *All* countries have ritual games. Child folklore or mythology plays a great part. Acting out of 'phobias' – purging themselves. Does the child play 'out' or play 'in' fears? e.g. teacher and cane. Does one reinforce old fashioned image of policeman, teacher, etc. by acting it in? Has one really got rid of it? 'Coming to terms' is a far better phrase than 'acting it out'. It could well be that as we have eliminated rituals from life, e.g. May Day, Rose Day, etc. children are fulfilling a need of their own, e.g. acting Spring and Winter ritual. Children love masks – over and over again they feel the need to act the same thing. *Vertigo* games – swing around etc. is this a surrender, a throwback to savage days?

It was unanimously decided that if one wants improvised Drama it is necessary to begin with the four-year-old children.

It is a presumptuous statement to assert that if there were no Drama people would not mature – but it can be said that one matures much more completely if one has encountered Drama. Drama can help one to become much better adjusted to life. Both English and Drama provide children with opportunities for doing things which they might not otherwise do, e.g. making papier maché masks which is frowned upon in a nice, clean, tidy home! The film of mental defectives climbing shows up the things they haven't done at home and this – though in less extreme cases – is seen frequently in children's play and all this contributes to show up the deficiency in the family. One can frequently see from the things they play what are their needs. Educational Drama can be structured so that children can go back and fulfil their real needs and maybe release them. Elements of Adult Drama are found in children's play and vice versa. There is a great need for a common language.

DISCUSSION GROUP NO. 6(b)
LEADER: D. H. GREEN

IMPROVISATION WITH SPECIAL REFERENCE TO GROWTH IN CHILDREN

General Discussion

The experience of most of the group was in secondary teaching and discussion centred mainly on this age range. The group were not troubled by any confusion between theatre and drama. In teaching, they worked satisfactorily on the basis of two kinds of related activities: work which was purely personal, whether group or individual, with no outside reference, and work which was conceived to some extent with a reference outside the group or individual in mind – an audience of some form. The first type of work was regarded as drama, the second as theatre, though the attachment of such labels came more as a result of the conference presenting such words than as a prior distinction by members of the group. Personal dramatic work would flow into performance or sophisticated theatre presentation if the children felt the need to do this. Often, both types of work would proceed at the same time.

The group welcomed professional or amateur productions in school, provided there was a good standard of presentation. Ideally, a number of points were looked for: participation by the school audience in some form; a play or programme related to the children's situation which could be followed up afterwards perhaps in various lessons; in general, drama which could fit into an existing pattern of work in the school. The group recognized however, that in many situations, it would rarely be possible to have such ideal arrangements and most members thought that the straightforward performance of a suitable play had value, even if only as a contrast to passive television viewing.

The group felt that drama as a teaching technique had a part to play in a wide range of the curriculum. They felt that a drama specialist was of considerable value on a school staff to establish a clearly conceived format of drama in special lessons and to advise and encourage other members of staff, especially specialist teachers of English. They were aware, however, of two particular problems. A drama teacher might advise on, and set an example of, a variety of approaches, but many teachers are unwilling to experiment in the more pupil-centred approach demanded by drama and it is no use expecting them to do this if they feel that such work is simply not suited to their personalities. The group thought also there was a danger that the drama specialist might preclude other people from trying dramatic work – the notion that all drama is the empire of the specialist can easily develop. The group welcomed the example of John Hersee as a mathematical specialist being in charge of the theatre and producing school plays and felt there was a value in this non-specialist approach which should not be lost. One might draw a parallel with the traditional attitude to games in boys' Grammar and Public schools where often nearly all members of staff assist with games, whether specially trained or not. It is nearly always expected of a new entrant to the profession in such a school that he does an afternoon on the games field. This often brings about a general interest in games on the part of the whole staff and an understanding of their value and difficulties. Some element of this general inter-disciplinary interest would be of great value in drama. Personally, I note with regret that in both Comprehensive schools in which I have taught, there has been a much stronger element of specialization in both games and drama.

Mention has been made of pupil-centred approach. The group felt that in this way, drama ran counter to the general ethos of much secondary school teaching. There was no external examination and rarely a structured syllabus comparable with those of most subjects. The drama teacher is much more concerned by virtue of his subject with the personal, emotional needs of the pupils than say the science or geography teacher, who is normally working through a syllabus to which the pupil has to adjust. This can mean there is little common ground between the approaches of different members of staff.

The group felt that a school play was valuable, but were emphatic that it should be related to drama work in the school and to the needs of the children. They resisted pressure from Heads, which they felt was common, to put on a school play as status symbol.

The group welcomed in-service training for teachers, especially short courses, even single day sessions on some limited topic. They felt, however, it was often difficult to encourage even English teachers to come to such courses and that it was easy for them to become the perquisite of a small in-group.

B. Special interest discussion

As a result of ideas opened up by the conference, the group did not stick very closely to this specific area. I will deal first with the points that were made in connection with drama and child development.

We felt that at the moment we could see no line of development in drama work specifically related to children's age and development – or only in very general terms. Much work is done in infant, junior and secondary schools that is really very similar. The group felt this did not matter, as children could develop to different extents, according to age, within a similar framework set by the teacher: different ages would explore and make use of different possibilities within the same theme or technique. Some members were not satisfied with this position, since we did not seem at all clear on what different uses were made of similar frameworks. We probably need to give more detailed attention to the role of drama at particular stages of development. The group, however, did not explore this area in detail, mainly because most members lacked experience with younger age groups.

The group did not feel that a syllabus in the traditional sense had any significance for drama teaching. The members did not teach according to any conscious line of development, rather they had a catalogue of skills and resources which they used according to what they felt were the needs of their pupils. One feels the situation would be more satisfactory if secondary teachers were given in training a more thorough understanding of child development so that the use of their skills could be made in the context of clearly understood principles instead of guess work and intuition. As a secondary teacher myself, I learned very little of child development or observing children and I believe this experience is not uncommon among graduate teachers. It is very easy in these circumstances to continue re-working a range of lessons, which is not satisfactory, even if one's repertoire is wide.

A number of points on the role of drama were generally accepted.

1. The lack of any drama, especially improvisation, or free discussion in the school curriculum was often demonstrated by inarticulate fifth and sixth formers. By implication the value of drama and related activities was shown.

2. Disturbed children and those with bad behaviour patterns can often be helped by drama work – perhaps because problems can be actively worked out in drama, perhaps because the relationship required between pupil and teacher to produce good drama is itself therapeutic.

3. It was important to allow some 'drop-out' in lessons – i.e. those who did not wish to participate should be allowed to do something else or watch and take part at a later stage.

4. Some structuring of drama work was important to help the child's natural sense of form. This might be done in various ways and for older pupils the structure could be fairly tight – a specific theme, story or situation, linked with consideration of theatrical art forms. For infants and juniors the structure would be much looser and more individual. There was always room for older pupils to have this much freer activity characteristic of younger children, provided this did not degenerate into an 'anything goes in drama' attitude. Several members spoke of having to combat this attitude, which prevented any educational value in the work.

Drama of adolescents was frequently a projection into adult life, with frequent knocks at authority figures (especially in schools with poor social environments). It was felt that not only could pupils work out aggressive feelings in this way, but the teacher could use the opportunity to help children understand the other side of the coin and gain insight into unfamiliar aspects of society.

There this report must end, rather in mid-air, as the discussion did.

DISCUSSION GROUP NO. 7(a)
                    LEADER: R. VERRIER

DRAMA IN RELATION TO THE TEACHING OF OTHER SUBJECTS[1]

The members of this group had a varied experience of employing drama as a tool in the teaching of subjects on the curriculum, but everyone felt a concern to explore ways in which drama could be made a more efficient tool in curriculum work.

A start was made by considering ways in which Colleges of Education helped students to use drama as a tool in their teaching of other subjects. The group heard of an interesting experiment at La Sainte Union College of Education, Southampton. A Creative Activities Course aimed at engaging students in a whole situation, i.e. one in which all the senses could be employed to apprehend an experience. For example, a sea shore may be explored by the students in their own way. Following this, discussion between students and tutors leads to a consideration of different ways in which the experience could be developed. Perhaps creative writing, poetry, historical or geographical research or investigation into Natural History may be suitable areas of development from which students make a choice. After research and preparation the students meet in a darkened room, broken by a central pool of light and present the results of their work to the rest of the group. The setting for the final presentation provides a dramatic experience even though no form of acting is necessarily involved. It was noted that experiments such as this one aimed at breaking through the traditional subject isolation in which context so much work is done at secondary level.

The group then considered more closely the role of drama in relation to other subjects and also some of the practical problems facing the non-drama trained teacher who may find himself in seven different and equally uninspiring rooms during the course of a day. It was suggested that drama could provide 'a garlic in the salad' in the teaching of other subjects. This is partly achieved because drama can provide a different approach to subject matter

[1] See Appendix IV for a description of an experiment in Drama and History.

normally presented verbally by the teacher or through course books. Drama functions also as a focal point at moments of climax. Reference was made to the way in which theatre illuminated 'the moments of conversion' in human experience. The challenge for the teacher is to discover the points of 'conversion' as they occur in the experience the pupils are going through – or even better, to use drama as the medium through which the pupils can make their own conversion.

At a practical level the group thought about the everyday problems of routine encountered in many secondary schools. In particular the problem of the forty minute period in a desk-populated classroom was considered. One member of the group showed how a large circle of white card placed on the floor or pinned to a blackboard could provide an imaginative dramatic focus, as can classroom lights, even in a room which cannot be blacked out. Other easily obtainable objects, which are also portable, include costume materials – stored by the teacher in his own room from which he can make a selection as the need arises; boxes of all kinds – suitably covered for different purposes; objects which produce sounds – a gong, to keys and chains; pictures of all kinds – especially helpful in setting a scene or to evoke a mood or character; and miscellaneous small personal effects which pupils themselves can provide. The group also mentioned the way in which desks could quickly be re-arranged to give additional levels of height and the necessary 'short-hand' suggestion of objects like cars or boundaries. All these points are probably obvious to the drama specialist, but the group felt that these suggestions are helpful to the subject specialist wishing to employ drama as a beginner in this skill.

It was generally agreed by the group that drama used in the teaching of other subjects does not mean subjecting the academic discipline to drama in such a way that the method swamps the academic content. Perhaps we have made a mistake in the past by demonstrating a use of drama which 'takes over' the academic discipline and leads away from rather than into the discipline. The group agreed that this was a very real danger. Would it prove possible to set up a number of experiments in which subject specialists in History, Maths, R.I., science, etc. combine with drama colleagues in order to discover how drama can function as a tool that can be discarded at any point in the lesson when research, writing or the narrative lesson are more appropriate to the needs of learning the discipline. A core problem is that of discovering, in conjunction with subject specialists, the particular conditions in which drama is the medium best suited to starting off an enquiry into a new topic, or the best medium to illuminate 'the moments of conversion'; or the best medium for clarifying what has been learnt or understood at the end of a lesson. The answers to these problems cannot be solved by the drama specialist and subject specialist.

It is hoped that experiments of the type described at La Sainte Union College of Education will eventually bring into the schools, teachers with a specialist knowledge of a discipline and also a working knowledge of drama as a medium of education.[1]

Finally the group would like to make a plea that the next conference of this type should include teachers of different disciplines as well as a greater representation of Head Teachers.

DISCUSSION GROUP NO. 7(b)
LEADER: J. MAYALL

DRAMA IN RELATION TO THE TEACHING OF OTHER SUBJECTS

General Discussion

The different approaches of the Presenters appear to have been chosen for convenience and clarity and we feel that they would not wish us to think of these aspects in isolation but as essential parts of the whole – Drama. All these parts provide variety which is desirable in the drama lesson; a balanced diet is essential.

Drama has much to offer the teacher in his task as a broad educator as well as a specialist. It widens the children's powers of expression provided that discussion plays a large part in it.

The School Play can be just a showpiece but it can be much more if the children are fully responsible for everything from lighting plots to discussion of characters and their interaction. The themes arising from the school play could well provide improvisation and discussion material for those not directly involved in its production. But enthusiasm does not last forever

---

[1] *Drama in Education* – A publication by the Institute of Education of Newcastle University provides some useful pointers for teachers wishing to employ drama as a tool in teaching other subjects.

and the wise teacher must know how to develop interest in new aspects and areas.

Exaggerated claims for drama are highly dangerous – we must use our sober judgement and not allow our enthusiasm to carry us away.

The production *Guns* was a good example of what properly handled drama can do, involving young people in a concern for the plight of others and in questioning the rights and wrongs of things. In this case drama became theatre. This need not happen and sometimes should not happen. The investigation of a particular problem may be private and personal to a group and may never be played to an audience.

The formal school production must not be dismissed out of hand. It has value provided the teachers see that value and use it fully. The majority of these formal productions tend to be *exclusive*, whereas classroom drama is *inclusive*. If the full educational value of the school play is to be realized then the school must have a good flexible attitude to both literature and drama. The disciplines imposed upon all taking part in the school play should be of value. A team working against a common adversary – the first night. The school play undoubtedly has many values but it should not be the only dramatic activity in the school.

We believe that it does require a certain type of person to make a good drama teacher, but can see no difference between him and the good teacher of any other subject. Both are using themselves and the children in an exciting adventure of investigation – an educational experience.

Where drama courses are provided for teachers they should be graded so that complete newcomers can be given the fundamental philosophy plus practical experience, and then move on to a more advanced level. Under the present system it is possible, unwittingly, to go on many beginners' courses and get no further on. Such courses should have a pattern of practical demonstration followed by discussion and should not omit information from the child psychologist where relevant.

Topic Discussion
The value of drama in relation to a subject depends upon the priorities surrounding, and often hedging in, that subject. The type of examination for which many of us train children forces us to adopt the teaching method which is the most efficient training

for answering examination questions. In this atmosphere drama is dismissed as being uneconomical use of time. However, the fact that examinations may be looming up should not mean shelving drama classes, as it is felt that drama involving logical thought and discipline will have some good effect in helping the children answer examination questions.

Not only does examination work make finding drama time difficult but the very timetable itself can prove a barrier. A flexible timetable would help things greatly. The 'activities' afternoon has much to commend it. The school building too is often unsuitable, causing an inhibiting consciousness that 'our noise might disturb the others'. To be able to work unseen and unheard is an essential step in educational dramatic development. But a little co-operation between members of staff can sometimes solve the problem of unsuitable rooms for drama, and the criticism of examinations should be balanced against the fact that many children do not take examinations at all. These children are fortunate in as much as they can make full use of drama in all subjects.

Can drama be used with all subjects? The answer to this is a reserved 'yes'. Its greatest *general* value is in its ability to capture children's interest, thus making research and the collecting of facts a pleasure. Its value as a teaching aid is undeniable, but it is only one of many ways of arousing interest and should not be forced on every class simply for the sake of it. Where a subject permits the child to take part in improvisation this *imaginative living experience* surely comes closer to reality, within the child, than any book, tape or film could. But for some subjects, like mathematics, there may be more appropriate teaching aids.

The Belgrade demonstration was felt to be a useful example of how visual aids, sound and drama can all be used with success to introduce a topic for further work by the class. English, History, Geography, Economic History, etc. all lend themselves to this treatment. To use this method in school would not be easy at the moment and would require a high degree of co-operation between subject teachers. Perhaps a dovetailing of departments is needed. The advent of team teaching may make this work easier.

One delegate felt, with regret, that the bias of the conference had been anti-academic. Even the questions suggested to guide discussion seemed loaded to make the group agree that drama is a panacea. His feeling was that drama is a stimulant and not a thinking discipline.

E

All would have liked more time to have been available for group discussion.

DISCUSSION GROUP NO. *10(a)*
LEADER: R. G. METCALF

ARE DRAMA AND THEATRE COMPATIBLE IN EDUCATION?

The first discussions, following up on the theme papers, were wide-ranging and, in writing this report, I have incorporated only those points which seem to me to be relevant to the group's topic for discussion. As for reaching a conclusion about the topic, this did not happen. After an initial discussion (Thursday) on the definition of Drama and Theatre, it was generally agreed that there was no great difference between them. What was beginning to emerge towards the end of the discussion period, and this must necessarily be a personal interpretation, was that there exists an important practical distinction between the two aspects.

It was felt that the demonstration by the Coventry Belgrade's Theatre in Education team aptly illustrated the difference between Drama and Theatre – that which took place in the seats (or in the classroom) being Drama; and that which developed from it (normally the performance in the school hall) being theatre. From this, Drama may be defined as something which takes place in the classroom or private, for educational purposes (i.e. the thing done) and Theatre as something which is shown by one group to another (i.e. the thing performed). Hence, logically, theatre would seem to grow out of Drama. The discussion returned to this point, asking whether it is sufficient to do something in the classroom, or whether to develop it into a performance (e.g. Lawrence Weston's *Guns*).

In the Belgrade demonstration, it was mentioned that they selected certain individuals, as a result of the classroom work, for 'parts', and it was felt by some members of the group that 'Theatre' was only for certain types of individuals (natural actors or exhibitionists?).

The first day's discussion spent some time on this question of performance, particularly in connection with the 'school play'. Should it be a performance of a scripted play, or develop from Drama work within the school? Indeed, should it take place at all? There seemed to be very little common ground here, but the following points did emerge:

(i) Scripted plays, if carefully chosen, can provide for possibilities inherent in the child; but,

(ii) It is quite possible to present such a play without the performers being aware of the meaning.

(iii) Theatre, even performance of scripted plays can, and desirably should, develop out of Drama in the school; although the participants need not be those doing Drama at the time.

This led to discussion of the value of school plays, both educationally and socially. Again very little common ground existed between the 'fors' and the 'againsts'; but whatever their educational value, it would be advisable not to forget that they do fulfil a useful social function, and not necessarily only for the performers.

At this point the discussion topic was considered again. Drama and Theatre had been defined, but surely the important term was 'Education'. On the meaning of this often debatable term, there was a large measure of common understanding, and it was agreed that this was the important point of the topic – not whether Drama and Theatre were incompatible, but whether they were so in education.

From this point the discussion moved to the training of Drama teachers, the skills they require and their place in the educational programme of a school. The point of the Colleges of Education was put. Students decide to take *Drama* because they are devotees of the *Theatre*, and it is therefore necessary to give them enough 'theatre' experience to get it 'out of their systems', and then to equip them with the different requirements of Drama in Education at different levels. It was also felt that the theatrical skills, particularly technical ones, did not take long to acquire and were useful in coping with the school play. One member of the group felt very strongly that this was not what Drama teachers were for.

This seemed to be one of the major problems of the present; although there was general agreement, in many circles, about the need for Drama teachers, it was not always certain what exactly they should be doing and, where the need was not agreed, it was not easy to make it felt. Being essentially practical only demonstration can achieve this. There is obviously need for more opportunities to see not only the work of professional theatre companies in the field of education, but also the sort of Drama work that is taking place in schools.

To proceed to the role of the drama teacher and of drama in a school. Firstly, it cannot be too strongly stressed that different aspects of drama are required at different stages in a child's education. At certain stages Theatre, as performance, could well be valid. In the first day's discussion, the idea of Drama as an 'educational methodology' was put forward, and later it was suggested that the theatre is a place where disciplines meet. It would seem that the Drama teacher could play an important part in team teaching, but Drama should not be considered only as a tool for teaching other subjects – in its own right it can be a valuable aid to integrating the individual. In a way the Belgrade's scheme is a form of team teaching. Might this not be an idea for future development – teams of professional actor/teachers working in a particular area in close association with schools. Certainly, if they were attached to theatres (although not necessarily paid by them) this would achieve the very desirable aim of integrating theatres into the community.

DISCUSSION GROUP NO. 11
LEADER: MRS S. THOMAS

DAY I

Our first discussion started with the presentation most immediate in our minds, The Professional Theatre in and for Schools.

We felt that the fact that money is being made available for this work is good, even when the result is not good, as it at least provides a starting point. The greatest factor in seeing that the result is good is the teacher's pastoral responsibility. The most valuable type of theatre/school relationship is that in which the team of actors get inside the community and learn about the needs of the people themselves before working out their productions.

This necessity for a viable point of contact is of even greater importance in the Drama work done in schools. It is essential for the teacher to start where the children are, whatever the intellectual or emotional level, whether they get their greatest involvement from the loud noise of pop-music, or from folk-music, from jungle-type dancing or wrestling. It was suggested that the urge towards such instinctive physical experiences is a healthy sign in the young, in that it is reaction against the sophistication and artificiality of our society today. One member of the group was doubtful of this and feared the danger of mob-hysteria, but in general we were more inclined to see this mass-emotion as a sort of ritual celebration of joys and fears.

This led on to the Lawrence Weston production *Guns*, a type of review presentation built up by members of the Sixth Form on the assassination of Robert F. Kennedy. There was a very wide divergence of views. In the general discussion provoked, some of the group queried the educational principle of Drama work being based on improvisation leading to the creation of the pupils' own theatrical production. They needed more than that which sprang from themselves. The value of working on the production of a good play by a proven dramatist was equally important. It was felt that even at the end of such an improvisation course, the pertinent question still needed to be asked from time to time by the teacher, to help the young actors think more accurately, and with more meaning for US HERE NOW.

One of our members believes that the only valid starting point for such improvisation is something directly concerning the young people themselves and within their own experience. But does there not come a time when work based on something that passionately interests them will have an extending and enriching power? They might perhaps find a relevant theme in one of the great stories of mankind and use it as a framework for their improvisation. One thinks of Jean Anouilh's *Antigone* written and produced in France under the German Occupation during the war. This type of approach and in particular the discipline of the study of the text of a play and its production, alternating with the improvised, helps towards greater clarity of thought.

Time was up, and we hadn't as much as thought about the other presentations.

DAY 2   DRAMA SPACES AND EQUIPMENT

'What is your opinion? You haven't said anything yet!' 'I don't know anything. I've come to listen and learn. I'm an architect'.

This is what got our main topic really going. First we had to find some common language. Not labels with their connotations, pleaded our architect but 'find out what happens and give it a name'. Too many bad theatres and studios were being built, and he wanted to start on his work in the right way.

We agreed that the time has come for real research into the whole field of Drama spaces and equipment in the light of future developments such as the raising of the school leaving age. The basic need is an empty space and people with ideas to fill it; the largest area possible should be provided, as smaller areas could be isolated by the use of lighting if needed.

Some people had found the windowless Withywood studio oppressive, and came back with second thoughts about the total exclusion of the outside world.

We arrived at a working compromise. Limited window-space placed high enough in the wall to prevent lookers in but at least giving a glimpse of the sky, and small enough to permit of complete black-out when required. The supplementary ventilation afforded can be very useful, as air-conditioning does not always deal with the extra heat generated by vigorously moving bodies.

A useful way of achieving variation in levels is for the main studio space to be in the form of a well, and using multi-purpose rostra. Some of this rostrumage could be used for the seating of an audience on the raised level surrounding the well, at times. It is useful to have ledges of shelves built as part of one of the walls and projecting from it, to serve as niches for displaying objects or for clambering on. It is important that the decor of such drama space should be neutral, but variation of texture could prevent any sense of drabness.

The relationship of the Drama space to a complete Art Block – we wanted all music rooms and drama studios to be sound-proofed. Movable walls for giving greater space as and when needed had one definite drawback, from a practical point of view, because of the difficulty of hanging of drapes or of lights.

A simple method of mobile lighting avoiding the danger of trailing flexes is made by Falks, a socket dimmer on a lighting gantry being designed for use by a child.

Rostra needed to be strong, rigid, yet light enough to be easily moved. Storing when not in use can present a problem. From this point of view, the best kind would seem to be made with framework sides, two opposite sides being hinged in the middle so that the framework will fold flat. The sides are held rigidly in position by the top, which is inserted as a lid and bolted home.

They have apparently this drawback after a certain amount of use, that the hinged side gets a bit rickety, and develops a creak.

Rostra need to be in various sizes and shapes, carefully planned in relation to each other, so that flights of steps, pillars, archways and ramps can be organized, as well as the building up of acting levels. Larger rostra could well be on casters or wheels, locked when in position to ensure immobility. All rostra should be capable of being bolted together to make a continuous stable surface when required. The lighting people, Furse, are very helpful in advising and making rostra.

For a Drama space large enough to be used also for a major production, and where money allowed, the type of flexibility of the Vandyke Theatre was interesting, but time did not allow us to expand the idea, nor even to talk about the theatre at the West of England College of Art, at Ashton Park.

DISCUSSION GROUP NO. 13(b)
LEADER: MRS A. MAVIUS

DRAMA IN THE PRIMARY AND MIDDLE SCHOOL

Group composed of 4 Primary School Teachers, 4 Prep. School Teachers, 2 Elocution/Drama part-time specialists, 1 student, 2 Teacher Trainers.

1. The group spent relatively little time defining and discussing Drama and Theatre as separate or conflicting ideas. It was fairly quickly agreed that the group's main interest was in what seemed to be generally known as Drama rather than Theatre because of its greater application to education in Primary and Middle Schools though Mrs K. Dowell, particularly, felt that Theatre and Theatrical experience was not out of place in Junior and even Infant Schools.

2. Some of the aims of using Drama in school were stated by the group to be:

   (a) Development of personality.

   (b) Development of imagination.

   (c) Development of awareness of the other's position and ability to empathize.

   (e) Fostering of group identification and working.

3. It was thought that for some children in some situations (e.g. very formal or rigidly timetabled schools) the aims mentioned above in (2) might be only attainable through Drama.

4. The group were agreed that continuity was very important and that if all teachers were trained to use Drama this would help to safeguard the children's opportunity for Dramatic experience. The part-time Drama specialists felt that in some respects it was easier to maintain continuity because they worked with the children throughout their school-life. Miss J. Chowen said that she had observed a markedly superior ease and fluency in speech and verbal communication in groups of children who had previously had a good deal of Drama experience in their classroom.

5. The group agreed on three main uses for Drama in the classroom:
   (i)   Drama as a Teaching Aid – e.g. Improvisation to 'make History real' or to stimulate creative writing.
   (ii) Therapeutically – e.g. playing out stressful situations or to encourage success attitudes in children not usually successful.
   (iii) As experience leading to Drama as an Art Form – e.g. the school play or as theatre.

6. The Primary School teachers saw the most important stimuli for Drama arising from a flexible minimally timetabled day in a classroom where good child/child and child/teacher relationships flourished in a trusting and supportive atmosphere. However, since Paradise is not always attainable everywhere other 'ways-in' to Drama which members of the group had found to be useful were listed:
   (a) Movement.
   (b) Music and songs.
   (c) Sounds and noise.
   (d) Stories.
   (e) Poems.
   (f) Objects (e.g. African beads).
   (g) Simple costume, e.g. wraps, cloaks, masks and boots and hats.
   (h) Experiences shared by members of the class or group.
   (i) Experiences especially meaningful (e.g. new baby) to individuals in the group.

7. The role of the Teacher was seen as:

(a) That of a stimulator and structurer of situations which would encourage the use of Drama by the children.

(b) Some members of the group saw the Teachers' role as a more active one in shaping the form and content of the dramatic work.

8. The group felt strongly that much more in-service training should be available to teachers. They asked that a resolution be put to the D.E.S. asking for better liaison and communication between the D.E.S. and L.E.A.'s so that teachers may be better informed about available courses. There was agreement that Drama should be a more important part of the normal teacher training as a separate subject but relating it to all work in junior and middle schools.

9. The question of whether Drama should be done in front of an audience was discussed. Mr R. J. Claypole said that he was coming to think that an audience was not a bad thing even in junior schools. Mrs P. Hall disagreed quite strongly with this view. It was thought that perhaps children choosing to 'do a play' for other children did not necessarily imply that the children wanted to perform to an audience so much as involve others in a peripheral way in their own group activity. The question of the child-produced service which often includes some Drama was brought up at this point.

10. The question of the School Play was raised. Mr M. T. Saville suggested that this called forth efforts which the children 'had not known they had it in them'. It was not generally thought to be a bad thing to have a School Play but some members of the group suggested that there were dangers, i.e. to exhibitionist personalities of which the teacher must be aware.

DISCUSSION GROUP NO. 14
LEADERS: J. DEWAR and B. HARVEY

VOICE AND SPEECH IN DRAMA

This group consisted of representatives of the primary school (2), the comprehensive (1), the public school (1), the College of Further Education (4) and also a County Drama Adviser and an English Adviser to a University Department of Education and a Private Practitioner (1).

Wednesday

We ranged widely over our field of interest, finding in our scrutiny much more to agree than to disagree about. We started by attempting to define the terms 'theatre' and 'drama', having a close look at the borderland between them. In the discussion that developed from that starting point the following seemed to us significant spheres of agreement:

1. Improvisation, mime, movement and speech are all important complementary aspects of educational drama and theatre.
2. Improvisation could be stultifying if it is kept within the limitations of the children's own experience; the teacher should aim at a widening of horizons either by his own probing, questioning and comment, or by leading them to the experience of literature – especially of course, dramatic literature.
3. Participation in a school or college play ('theatre'), if properly directed, was a valuable experience for the children concerned in it.
4. In-service training courses in educational drama were highly desirable to encourage more teachers to use the dramatic method.

More controversial views upheld by some of the group were:

1. Any good teacher can teach educational drama.
2. Those in the professional theatre (especially directors) may be better equipped to teach educational drama and/or theatre? than the professional teacher.
3. Movement is educationally valid for its own sake, and need not have an 'end product'.
4. The young people presenting *Guns* gave, in theatrical terms, a crude performance, and in the ensuing discussion showed some complacency and lack of modesty.
5. The 'send-up' of Lincoln's Gettysburg Speech by John Hodgson's pupils was considered by some members tasteless and pointless.

Thursday

'Voice and Speech in Drama'. The group, in dealing with the subject of their individual choice, again found themselves in general agreement. These were the main areas of discussion:

1. We felt that speech was so important an element, not only in educational drama, but in the whole field of education as a preparation for life, that it should have had separate treatment

by a conference speaker. As a single element of drama, and
still more of theatre, it was felt to be equally important with,
for instance, movement or improvisation.

2. We agreed that 'good speech' should be aimed at, and that it
entailed:

(*a*) a wide vocabulary, adequate for and suited to the occasion.

(*b*) good listening – a concentrated and courteous attention to
other speakers.

(*c*) such 'technical' considerations as clear enunciation and a
full and flexible use of the mechanism of speech.

3. In discussing 'accent' (by which we meant, broadly, local
variations in speech), we agreed on the following:

(*a*) local accents were in general acceptable, provided they
were intelligible to other speakers of English.

(*b*) We are all to some extent multi-lingual, adopting a different
'style' of speech and even a different 'register' – according
to the speech situation we are in.

(*c*) we deplore both the snobbery of those who consider S.R.P.
(Southern Received Pronunciation) the only 'correct' form
of English, and the inverted snobbery of those who find
nothing at all to be said for a form of English that is still
regarded throughout the world as 'standard' English.

4. We discussed the terms used by Bernstein, 'restricted code' and
'elaborate code', and agreed that in general an elaborate code,
with its wider vocabulary and subtler discrimination in meaning, should be encouraged.

DISCUSSION GROUP NO. 15(a)
LEADER: L. SMITH

General Discussion
Discussion began on the problem of definition, but with a realization that valuable time could be used up in this way. Thus the
following definitions were accepted quickly but are not put
forward as other than tentative working definitions:

(i)   Drama = conflict;

(ii)   Theatre = mastery of techniques to produce an effect on an
audience;

(iii)   Education = development of the personality as far as
possible.

With these in mind, the lectures and demonstrations we had heard and seen were considered. Three topics especially engaged our attention.

1. *Documentary Drama*

We wondered whether there was a tendency to exaggerate the 'sociological' approach to drama, following what was a current fashion. As such, it was considered a valuable lead-in to drama as to other subjects, but we wondered if there were elements in such work which were in some way at war with other, more important, elements in drama.

2. *Improvisation*

Several members of the group had used improvisation leading towards a text (e.g. *As You Like it*) in order to get pupils emotionally involved in the themes they would meet. We wondered if the *discussion* involved in this were not perhaps more important than the actual dramatic process. Eventually there was a realization that the playwright had done it better. This led us to consider the importance of form, which we thought should always be an aim, but need only be an *awareness* of form induced by the teacher, which will anyway arise from the children (e.g. how to end?). More conventionally, awareness of form can come through a finished production or the discovery that a text by Shakespeare organizes emotion expertly. Some members of the group wondered if this kind of improvisation, or any kind of drama, was equally valuable for all ages, intelligences and abilities; in the school situation, some selection was often necessary.

Another use of improvisation made by members of the group had been the construction of a play *after* reading a text, e.g. *Our Town* becomes *Our Street*.

3. *Movement*

Several had been strongly impressed by the 'Movement' demonstration. They found it difficult to see this clearly related to drama though it was obviously a valuable hand-maiden. It seemed to have more significance, however, as true Physical Education.

Two other areas were covered in the remainder of the discussion: Drama as a school subject, and visits by or to the theatre.

We thought it impossible to generalize about the job of a drama specialist, which could vary from school to school. Similarly we felt unable to say that drama should be compulsory, or optional, or an alternative to games. The whole question of the curriculum was too massive a subject to pursue; its complexity was especially realized when we touched on subject integration, in that drama as a new specialism at first seems to run counter to modern methods of organizing the curriculum.

Finally we saw visits by or to a theatre as to some extent balancing the modern habit of stressing creativity. Children need to be taught how to be an audience. How should plays be selected? It was generally felt that if there were a danger in children seeing 'unsuitable' plays, it was minimized by the therapeutic effect of discussion afterwards. A member of the group had taken young children to see *King Lear*; they had been shocked, but in discussion afterwards revealed a deep understanding.

WRITING AS THE OUTCOME OF DRAMA

The topic gave rise to wider discussion about stimuli for writing, about the good and bad influence of television in forming concepts of character and form, and about the relationship between drama and music.

The following points are extracted as being the most relevant to the topic.

1. There were examples of script-writing stimulating less able pupils to be creative.
2. The process could be:
   (a) discuss and act: character in situation;
   (b) decide and act: sequence of events;
   (c) discuss, evolve and write script.
3. Derivative material (T.V. or text) was considered valid if translated to known circumstances.
4. Acting could be used to test, modify, rewrite a script.
5. The 'Circus' situation had proved valuable, especially with remedial children; it provided opportunities for individual or group work, and writing of many kinds, e.g. the story of the circus, or the life-story of one character.
6. T.V. scripts were thought too complex, thus inhibiting to imitate. Better methods were the 'idiot-board' technique (similar to a comic-strip) or 'Photoplay' (Kodak pamphlet).
7. Improvisation can make one feel so strongly that one wishes to make the result permanent in the form of a script. Here the intellect comes to bear on the emotional impact of an improvisation, But
8. Improvisation can be primarily for that one moment in time –

scripting it, or playing a tape-recording of it can kill. Obviously, the teacher must decide at the time.

DISCUSSION GROUP NO. 15(b)
LEADER: J. KNEE

WRITING AS THE OUTCOME OF DRAMA

1. In the classroom Drama has an immediacy that the other Arts lack, e.g. it can arise out of boys wrestling on the floor by the simple expedient of introducing an imaginary T.V. camera to which they can respond.
2. The bogey of examinations. Does it really exist? As practising teachers, we felt that examinations can be the shield behind which 'the teacher who does not wish to do it' can hide.
3. A general feeling that a great deal of lip service is paid to Drama in schools but that, in fact, very little is done.
4. Training institutions are under-equipped to deal with Dorothy Heathcote's ideas.
5. It ought to be appreciated that Movement is the basic form of communications, e.g. 'I walk towards you' may be a menace. 'I run from you' may mean 'I am afraid of you'.

On the Thursday morning discussion 'Writing as the Outcome of Drama' there seemed to be general agreement that writing could arise from Drama but that it had no special value as a stimulus. Prose or poetry could be equally well employed for this purpose.

It was generally felt that Drama is an end in itself.

DISCUSSION GROUP NO. 16A
LEADER: D. WEEKS

IMPROVISATION WITH SPECIAL REFERENCE TO PLAY PRODUCTION

As this group was convened to talk about 'Improvisation with special reference to Play Production', we started by discussing

John Hodgson's talk on 'Improvisation and Literature'. Some people in the group felt it worked well with talented students but found it difficult to see themselves in the role of a teacher with a class of 30-plus to contend with. What, they wanted to know, were the controls a teacher had over his group and how quickly did the children assimilate improvisation techniques?

This brought us on to the first real problem. Many of the group taught in rather formal grammar schools where tremendous academic pressure was exerted. Since the parents wanted examination success at all costs great difficulty arose about the inclusion of Drama in the curriculum; whether it should be merely a vehicle towards examination success by its furtherance of a child's interest in literature, or whether it should do all the other things which serious drama teachers know it can.

Where then should Drama be started in this sort of situation? Some advocated a start in the Sixth Form as a voluntary activity perhaps with a performance of some kind in mind, others thought it should be started in the first year and be allowed to grow. The Head's role in this, and the personality of the teacher was all-important.

To help to start and, indeed, further dramatic work it was suggested that students should be invited to work with a class under the supervision of the Drama teacher. The visits of Theatre companies were discussed and unanimously welcomed. It was suggested that there should be more regular meetings between the companies and teachers to discuss the needs of individual schools and the need for specialist touring actor/teachers was stressed, an impression much strengthened by the work of the Belgrade Company at the Conference.

Having agreed that Drama was a desirable addition to the syllabus in schools and colleges, we went on to discuss its value. All agreed that Improvisation made children more aware of themselves – their powers of observation and sensitivity increased, but a warning note was sounded about their awareness of other people. A lot of Drama work seems to be about *myself*. Group relationships and an understanding of social problems were considered essential to the development of drama teaching.

The usual problems were aired about the level of noise accepted by oneself and others, about teachers not trained for drama work taking lessons, staff and Head's hostility, ignorance and philistine attitudes, and suitable facilities, especially an appropriate room.

The integration of drama with other subjects and the importance of its use in other subjects was another topic of concern, and the rift in many schools between arts and sciences is still very wide.

Having talked in general terms and aired views and grievances, we then went on to talk about our specific subject.

We talked first about improvised plays and looked at several prompt copies and described how these plays are built up from factual information and gradually fitted into a framework of the subject matter. Research was all-important here and the teacher's role was to be a sort of walking reference-book on all aspects of the problem covered. He should be able to direct pupils to certain books, records, films, etc., and should have a clear idea of how the information, when compiled, should be used. His real skill lies in the communication of all the material collected in a coherent form to the audience. For this a wide knowledge of different theatrical techniques is necessary. The value in this sort of work lies in the involvement of the children in the play and the depth of understanding they bring to the material. A well-improvised play can bring a degree of articulation to the participants which they would otherwise certainly not acquire.

From improvised plays we next looked at the use of Improvisation in understanding a scripted play. The danger of imposing a different, even contradictory mood and situation was brought up and it was essential for the teacher to prepare himself thoroughly. In some cases it might be valid to imagine the situation before the play began and improvise it to provide background knowledge for the actors. Two main approaches were considered – whether to improvise a theme relevant to the play before the children read it or to read the play first and then explore its meaning. It was felt that generally the first approach would be ideal for younger children and certainly for many older ones, whilst the second would be for more mature pupils.

As the Bretton Hall students joined our group we asked them to do some practical work with us so that we all had a common experience to discuss. We chose *Death of a Salesman* as a play with great depth and contemporary relevance and, indeed, one which is on some 'A' level syllabuses.

We took certain scenes and tried to see whether improvisation helped to illuminate the text and whether we could understand the play better as a result of it. Some groups tried improvising situations, others discussed the meanings and ideas. Everyone found that closer study in small groups was far more interesting, and those who tried improvising said that it helped them to see more clearly what the scene was about and how the characters thought and felt. Questions were raised about the time it would take to use this approach for examination work but it was generally agreed that its effectiveness would outweigh the time taken, each play becoming progressively more quickly understood.

We then looked at improvisation as an aid to play production. We discussed its use in understanding the 'undertext' and thought processes. We agreed that improvisation didn't suit all play directors but that it should be used far more often, particularly in situations where an impasse arises over a difficulty of interpretation in rehearsal. Improvising a character's reactions to different situations was a valuable aid to deepening an actor's awareness of his role and of the relationships between himself and other characters in the play. The director had a great responsibility in taking care that improvisation did not minimize or lose the author's words in performance. There was some dispute about having books in hand during rehearsal. Was it really possible to abandon them, or merely a pious hope? In either case to rehearse with book in hand, except during the early stages of rehearsal was found to be unnecessarily inhibiting.

In sum, improvisation had many uses. Far too many people are unaware of its value and, having talked a great deal about many of its applications, we should all now be prepared to do something about it.

DISCUSSION GROUP NO. 16(b)
LEADER: MRS J. WILKINSON

IMPROVISATION LEADING TO PLAY PRODUCTION

No final conclusions were reached, although there was general agreement that improvisation can help towards play production in various ways. These include:

(a) Introduction to difficult texts by setting up a situation within the children's own experience, at first or second hand, which is allied to the action of the play. An example was given of an introduction to *Trojan Women* by using an improvisation about Vietnam women in the present war.

(b) Improving bad translations of plays by putting the text into modern idiom.

(c) Continuing by improvisation modern 'incomplete' plays which have no definite ending.

(d) The development of character and relationships.

(e) Helping children to work together, improving their reactions to situations, and their ability to listen to and assimilate the ideas and feelings of other people, so that they work as a team and not as individuals.

Several problems were raised, one being the difficulty of breaking down the dramatic inhibitions of some intelligent children who seem embarrassed by physical expression. An example of this was given by one delegate who found difficulty with quiet, well behaved children in dealing with violence. With such children it may be helpful to begin with discussion and lead on to action when they feel ready for it.

The group agreed that there were dangers in the over-use of improvisation, e.g. that it could possibly dull the immediate intellectual reaction to, and appreciation of a text because of the need for association. Also that teachers should know their own 'thresholds' (to borrow Mrs Heathcote's phrase) and not lose control of the improvisations. It was agreed that the teachers should be involved with the work of the children and not just act as observers. The relationship between teacher and pupils is of paramount importance, as no productive drama work can be done where there is any sense of personal aggression or strain.

The group heard a fascinating account of the work done in the Special Unit of the Bristol Detention Centre. Here the use of Drama is entirely therapeutic and based on the treatment of the delinquent, with the teacher being entirely one with the children and actually playing with them in their improvisations and where there is the added difficulty of a lack of access to external experience. The plays are unscripted as a majority of the children are illiterate. The obvious dedication and enthusiasm in the teaching was a tremendous example to the rest of the group and made us realize that what we considered to be real problems are very minor in comparison.

DISCUSSION GROUP NO. 16(c)
LEADER: D. HALE

IMPROVISATION WITH SPECIAL REFERENCE TO PLAY
PRODUCTION

2.4.69

Drama/Theatre. Does improvisation lead on naturally to 'theatre'?
Comments on *Guns* as being obviously 'theatre' – in fact it seemed
to have taken a subject and hung it upon an existing (and somewhat polished) theatrical technique. Disadvantage of teacher not
being involved – there was an obvious horizontal development,
where the right questions could have produced vertical development. It was apparently evolved with an audience always in mind
– therefore it was 'theatre' from the start.

Movement for Drama. The teacher must always be aware of his
aims. Is there a difference between Movement and Movement for
Drama? For movement work such as Mrs Sherborne describes
a specialist is needed.

Drama Specialist. It was felt that there was a definite need for
drama specialists, who should work in full co-operation with
teachers of other subjects.

Drama Syllabus. Some felt that this was desirable, but all agreed
that it was very difficult in practice. There is a need for guidance
for interested but inexperienced or untrained teachers.

Other Points. There was a strong desire for practice, and observing
of Drama teaching – to see the Speakers in action. Courses only
provide a starting point. Workshops for Drama Teaching – help of
Theatre in Education teams. Positive attitudes to Drama and Movement must be established early – certainly by Junior level. The
traditional image of the teacher can be inimical to Drama work.

1. Courses needed for Head Teachers as introduction to Drama.
2. Training colleges are too academically biased – not enough
   actual continuing contact with children.
3. More link between the junior and secondary schools – secondary schools should be able to take over and develop the basic
   drama/movement work done in junior schools.
4. Conference needed with more concentration on work actually
   done in schools – 'drama' work rather than work with a strong
   theatrical element.

5. Theatre in Education work is needed with teachers as well as with pupils.

3.4.69

Improvisation is a valuable method for approach to and introduction to a play, in rehearsal or in classroom – variation on theme, different contexts. It is more an exploration of the theme, situations, characters, rather than of the text itself. Improvisation must be relevant to the children's experience; if it is also relevant to the text it will aid understanding – it can put things into the children's own terms. Improvisation can go out of the text and explore what happens before and after the action contained in the text. Young children 'copy' – and an amalgam of copied characteristics can produce something original. The child will explore his own character rather than another's. Improvisation can be used purely as a loosener or mood-creator at the beginning of a rehearsal session. Improvisation can be a great aid to teamwork. A conventional approach to a scripted play can often isolate the small parts, and also many characters become unaware of how they fit into the rest of the play – they often only know anything about the scenes that they are actually in. Improvisation work before and during play develops a group feeling and sensitivity. The actors realize that they are all part of a whole and that the small parts are all important. Improvisation can be invaluable during rehearsal – to deal with awkward crowd scenes, or a difficult duologue. Improvisation can be used as a safety valve if a rehearsal session is not sufficiently relaxed.

DISCUSSION GROUP NO. 17(a)
LEADER: W. REES

DRAMA AS A BASIC OR CURRICULUM COURSE IN COLLEGES OF EDUCATION

All members of the group, apart from one, were members or staff of Colleges of Education.

The terms 'basic' and 'curriculum' had different meanings in different colleges but for the purpose of our discussions it was agreed that 'basic' would be applied to a course followed by all students (if such a course existed in that college) and 'curriculum' be used to describe a course, not necessarily followed by all students, which would be concerned with teaching methods and classroom techniques.

There was general agreement that the contribution of drama (in this sense, largely unscripted and improvised) to the development of the student was of such importance that all students in Colleges of Education should have drama as part of their course. This was particularly important for students who were preparing to teach in Primary Schools. Drama should include movement; also the quality of the student's speech should receive particular attention. There was insistence that no attempt should be made to impose a standard pronunciation but that the work should aim for clarity and ease and enjoyment of communication.

Students taking English as a Main Subject should receive extra tuition and practice with children to make them competent in the use of classroom drama so that they would be in a position, as members of school staffs, to act as leaders in this work.

The strong sense of disquiet amongst members of the group with the present position in Colleges of Education stemmed mainly from problems concerned with the following:

1. *Staffing.* Work in speech and drama could not be adequately covered when, for example, one member of staff is responsible for 900 students. Either more specialist staff have to be appointed or members of other departments have to be encouraged to help. Groups were generally too large (35 to a group in one case when 20 students to a group should be the maximum for this work).

2. *Accommodation.* Few colleges have space reserved for this work. In most cases, cramped lecture rooms were the only spaces available and equipment had to be cleared at the end of each period. Drama needs space and it seems that schools are generally better equipped in this respect than Colleges of Education.

3. *Time.* The time available for speech and drama is generally inadequate. A 50-minute period a week, which seemed the most general, is not enough to cover the needs of both speech and drama.

DISCUSSION GROUP NO. 17(b)
                  LEADER: E. MALINS

DRAMA IN COLLEGES OF EDUCATION

All but one member of this Group were lecturers in Colleges of Education.

Although the details of our Drama courses varied widely from College to College we were unanimous in our aims, which we felt it would not be profitable to discuss further. In short, these were (a) the development of the student as a person, and (b) his being equipped to practise the teaching of Drama in schools, with a full understanding of its role in the general educational pattern. We therefore concerned ourselves with discussions concerned with practical matters, and in these we were able to come to certain unanimous conclusions despite the variety in our Courses.

A. *Recommendations for College of Education Drama Courses*
1. *Teaching Practice.* It was felt that Drama on Teaching Practice should not be encouraged, especially on the first Practice. The lack of confidence which a student could easily experience through failure to achieve successful improvisation or other dramatic activity under these artificial conditions was not worth the risk. It was thought to be impossibly hard for students to try to deal with problems with children whom they had not yet grown to know. Assessment should therefore never be made on such activities on Teaching Practice.
2. *Speech.* The attainment of a confidence in oracy should receive continuous attention from the moment a student takes up the Course. Only through this confidence can he be a successful teacher of Drama or any other subject. This particular training should not be confused with formal speech training, which was thought to be unnecessary or undesirable.
3. *Movement.* This was also thought to be an integral part of the Course, and again not with a highly specialist training, but acquired naturally through good improvisation.
4. All students should receive thorough training in audio/visual equipment and light/sound apparatus. An increase in the usually inadequate number of Technical Assistants in most Colleges would help in this respect.
5. Students should be encouraged to have wider contacts with

communities outside the Colleges. In these they could gain valuable experience in Drama in Youth Clubs or Play Groups.

B. *Relationships between schools and colleges of education.*
1. These should be encouraged so that more visits take place between these two parties. Through visits to Colleges, teachers may begin to realize some of the practical difficulties currently suffered in Drama training, through lack of equipment, inappropriate accommodation or unsuitable timetabling.
2. Teachers, and especially Head Teachers, may also discover after visits to Colleges some of the aims of a Drama course and its importance in the curriculum at all ages.
3. Similarly, more visits to schools, with reciprocal Drama possibly arranged, may obviate the present situation, which is often too common, whereby a specialist student in Drama finds on arrival as a trained teacher that he is relegated, by a Head unsympathetic to Drama, to the teaching of English or other subjects.

Summing-up

IT WILL BE CLEAR from the reports that there is considerable agreement that drama is an important part of the educational experience which ought to be available to all children, but that there is still much thinking and work that needs doing. After the first discussion session on the role of drama and theatre in education, groups were invited to put forward some of the most important topics which need further thought and development: these topics included: the role that drama could play in I.D.E. schemes in the early years of secondary schooling; the place of drama in the training of teachers; the ways in which actors and teachers can best help each other; the place of specialist teachers and specialist knowledge in drama work; the importance of purpose, form and control in improvisation; the difficulties created for certain types of drama by the subject dominated timetable of most secondary schools; the place of external examinations in drama e.g: Mode III C.S.E. and combined Drama and English 'A' level courses; the great need for different kinds of in-service training; the desirability of teachers in many specialisms having an awareness of what is needed in drama work.

All these points and many others, require thought, work and development, and there was no doubt that many amongst those who attended the Clifton College Conference were anxious to harness their enthusiasm to clear thinking and practical action.

Finally, the editors would be glad to hear of any work related to the concern of the conference that has taken place since Easter 1969 and would be glad to put interested people in touch with members of the Clifton Conference who may live in their area.

APPENDICES

Appendix I

Programme of Conference

---

*DRAMA AND THEATRE IN EDUCATION –
CLIFTON COLLEGE CONFERENCE EASTER 1969*

*A National Conference Monday March 31 – Thursday April 3,
sponsored by Bristol Education Authority, Bristol Old Vic Company
and Clifton College.*

> *What needs to be done is not to define the
> frontiers of a subject where no frontiers
> exist, but to establish clearly the contri-
> bution of dramatic activity to the growth
> and education of children.*
> (Drama: Education Survey 2, Department
> of Education and Science, p. 90)

AIMS AND PATTERN OF CONFERENCE

The Conference will look critically at the different kinds of activity embraced by 'drama and theatre in education' and the claims made for them.

It will be of interest not only to practitioners but also to those responsible for curriculum policy, such as heads of schools.

It will be relevant to the work of all teachers, those involved in teacher training and those professionally concerned with the theatre.

Phase One: Awareness
The Conference will start with a survey of current practice and thinking, and in order to sharpen the focus of the discussions, Tuesday will be devoted to the presentation by practitioners of a

variety of approaches through description, demonstration, visual illustration, film, tapes and other appropriate means. In addition to creating awareness of practice, the presenters will attempt theoretical justification of the educational merits of what they are doing and ample time will be given for the raising of questions designed to clarify 'Aim, Method and Content'.

Phase Two: Analysis
The second phase of the Conference will begin on Wednesday, 2 April, when the Conference will break up into groups for critical discussions arising from the Tuesday sessions. On Thursday, 3 April, the first session will give each group an opportunity to discuss one aspect more thoroughly.

Conclusion
It is appreciated that no final answers should be given to the questions that this Conference will be considering; but in the closing session it is hoped that there will be some positive suggestions for further investigation and development, not only by members of the Conference but also in the fields of teacher-training and in-service training.

OUTLINE PROGRAMME AND SPEAKERS

MONDAY 31 MARCH
Tea
'Drama and Theatre in Schools: a critical Survey' – Gavin Bolton, Durham University Institute of Education.
Dinner
Civic reception by the Lord Mayor of Bristol, Councillor Mrs Mercia Castle.

TUESDAY 1 APRIL
Breakfast
'Improvisation and Literature' – John Hodgson, Bretton Hall College of Education.
Coffee
'The Use of Drama in Teaching' – Dorothy Heathcote, Newcastle University Institute of Education.
Lunch
'The School Play' – John Hersee, Clifton College.

'The Professional Theatre in and for Schools' – Mark Woolgar, Bristol Old Vic.
Tea
'Movement and Drama' – Veronica Sherborne, External Examiner in the Art of Movement, London University Institute of Education.
Dinner
Guns, a play created by sixth formers of Lawrence Weston School.

WEDNESDAY 2 APRIL
Breakfast
Group discussion initiated by Gavin Bolton.
Lunch
Visits to theatres, drama studios, etc., technical demonstrations.
Tea
Demonstration programme by the Theatre in Education Team, the Belgrade Theatre, Coventry.
Dinner
Opportunity to attend one of Bristol Old Vic Company's current productions.

THURSDAY 3 APRIL
Group discussion on selected subjects.
Summing up by John Allen, H.M.I. – responsible for the D.E.S. Drama Survey.
Reception by the Headmaster of Clifton College, Stephen McWatters, followed by *Lunch*.

VISITS, EXHIBITIONS, DEMONSTRATIONS

Accommodation, equipment and expertise are important aspects of certain branches of drama and theatre education. There will be a wide range of exhibitions, a display of texts and demonstrations of lighting, make-up and the design of drama studios and theatres, examples of which will be visited.

STEERING COMMITTEE

For Bristol Education Authority
Winifred Hickson, Inspector of Schools, Bristol.

For the Bristol Old Vic
Mark Woolgar, Bristol Old Vic, Assistant Producer with special responsibility for schools.
For Clifton College
John Hersee, Master in charge of the School Theatre.
Nigel Dodd, Head of the English Department, and Conference Secretary.

Appendix II

Presenters' Papers and Theme Papers

---

1. THE USE OF DRAMA IN TEACHING

No one ever teaches a teacher how to do the job. He becomes able to fill the role – however comfortably or hamfistedly – by a process of attrition, trial by fire and experience. Presumably a personal need to inform others about his absorbing interests makes him attracted to the profession and keeps him in it once he is launched. And he either must sink or swim. Usually the latter happens because he must establish – however blindly – his positions of comfort which allow him to manoeuvre, and the way he fulfils the teacher role in the long run is based upon these comfortable thresholds. He also has one other problem – he rarely understands the process he employs to make vivid and interesting the material which interests him, so he spends his life blindly trying to cause the same miracle which happened to him, to happen to others. What makes history 'live' for some? How is the inner life of the written word revealed to the potential teacher of literature? What attractions have young children which make them material for study and effort? All of us can hazard a guess but in the long run every person must do it for himself.

Presumably at some stage a teacher role emerges after a certain number of experiences good and bad, rewarding and fearsome, have been absorbed into the system. So he becomes 'jelled' into his particular teacher-type, at once a common phenomenon yet unique in that there is only ever one quite like him. He also reaches a stage, if he is lucky, when he is able to take stock and examine his methods, aims and principles in relating to children and to modify them fruitfully.

For example, he may examine what it is which causes him to keep on, day after day, re-entering the same difficult form-rooms and struggling to make communication. In my saner greyer moments I shake my head at my stupidity - till I remember again the thrills of spending my days structuring situations for others of the kind I delight in myself.

This is not intended to be cynical – any of it. It is an urgent desire to penetrate into the teacher-mystique. If communication is to be achieved with others of one's kind it is imperative that this be done if only so that courses can be better structured.

If Drama is to be understood as an educational matter requires to be, then it must be related to the above, i.e. the personality of the individual teacher and his methods of work, *and* to the needs of his classes, *and* lastly to the requirements of the medium itself. This latter must not be ignored. It nearly always is. So we are concerned with three main areas: the medium; the teacher-type; the needs of the children.

The medium is very simple, and extremely difficult. Briefly it happens when *Persons now conflict*. Therein lies its simplicity. The difficulty lies in grasping the infinite variety of its phenomena and the fact that it only ever exists in the 'now-ness' of the experience for those who are currently in its thrall. One art form is only expressed in another by a process of radical change so to try to capture Drama in words is doomed before we begin.

The teacher-type can however be put in a position where he may begin to understand (*a*) *whether* he can use this area of experience in his teaching, and (*b*) *how* he would make use of it.

Out of these considerations he can be in a position to chart his course and be in command of the medium – provided he can appreciate its nature and disciplines. Otherwise he remains its slave unable to make it work for him.

The needs of children are becoming ever more apparent to us. Perhaps one day they may be considered in our planning of schools and the minutiae of the environment, curriculum and results we demand of them?

These areas will be the subject of my talk.

DOROTHY HEATHCOTE

2. *MOVEMENT AND DRAMA*

Movement is becoming accepted as a necessary and integral part of dramatic experience. Movement and voice are both physical expressions of the person, and the way one moves will be reflected in the way one speaks. The teacher tries to help the child find both physical and vocal freedom.

In order to acquire a rich movement vocabulary one tries to develop a greater awareness of the body itself; the trunk, limbs, hands, feet, head and face can all be immensely expressive. Awareness of the infinite variety of ways of moving help people to have more control over *how* they move.

This awareness demands concentration, the capacity to be physically and mentally focussed on the job in hand. Embarrassment and self-consciousness are the main hurdles to overcome in movement classes with beginners, and perhaps the only way to do this is to emphasize the physical and practical aspects of movement to start with.

Movement is not an end in itself; it can be geared towards gymnastics, dance or drama. For any of these activities it is helpful if the individual is well centred, physically, in himself, and well based, physically, on the ground. Being centred and 'earthed' provide a good starting point for dramatic work. There are as many ways of moving as there are people, one hopes to help children become more aware of how they move, as well as more aware of how they could move. As well as stretching the members of the class in many directions one encourages every sign of inventiveness, initiative and imagination.

Apart from the generally broadening effect movement can have, it also has a specific contribution to make when the acting of a character in a play is the main consideration.

It is easier for a producer if the actors are at home in their bodies, understand what tension really means, understand how to move in spatial terms, have a feeling for rhythm, and so on. It is interesting to see how an actor adapts his own movement patterns to the way of behaving and moving of the character he is portraying.

Movement opens many doors, it increases understanding of something we take for granted and often neglect, and it gives a discipline and technical control which is valuable in interpreting character in plays. Perhaps its most valuable contribution comes through improvisation when groups of people create something satisfying and meaningful for themselves.

QUESTIONS

1. What do we mean by movement – Laban movement, body movement, dramatic movement?
2. Should the teacher go through a course of training in movement before attempting to teach it?
3. Where does one find such a course?
4. Is there a tendency for the teacher to train the class to move in a style similar to his own?
5. Is it possible for specialists in P.E., dance, and dramatic movement to work along the same lines?
6. Can a teacher do useful movement work in the classroom, or is a hall or gym essential?
7. How does one help children to get over embarrassment and self-consciousness to a point where they can be really involved?

VERONICA SHERBORNE

3. THE SCHOOL PLAY

1. The two characteristics which distinguish this subject from the activities called 'Drama' are:
   (i) it is concerned with a performance before an audience.
   (ii) generally it is an extra-curricular, voluntary activity.
2. Types of performance include: rehearsal improvisation; revue; dancing; opera; a scripted play which may be:
   (i) a play by a professional playwright from Sophocles to Speight,
   (ii) a script written by a teacher, perhaps modified as rehearsals progress,
   (iii) a script written and developed by the pupils.
   The scripted play written for professional performance is the traditional school play and this will be the main concern, but the other types of performance all have elements in common with it, especially the intention to communicate with the audience, as well as amongst the performers.
3. Reasons for performing a School Play.
   (i) Pleasure
   (ii) Awareness of others, their characters and situations
   (iii) Self-awareness
   (iv) Discipline and self-discipline
   (v) Appreciation of the Theatre as an Art and of its Crafts
   (vi) A team activity
   (vii) An integrating activity which can involve many different sectors of the school
   (viii) Provided that no Department monopolizes the School Play it can be a liberalizing and vitalizing activity across many disciplines.
4. Theatre and Drama are not in conflict:
   (i) Many of their aims are the same.
   (ii) Drama lessons can contribute to the Play and vice versa.
   (iii) A performance requires extra skills.
   (iv) Working to a deadline, rehearsing to improve, the importance of each member of the 'team' all provide valuable stimulus and discipline.

JOHN HERSEE

4. *IMPROVISATION AND LITERATURE*

SPECIAL POINTS FOR DISCUSSION

1. Relationship between drama and literature – drama as literature – drama towards literature – drama out of literature.
2. Drama as a means of introducing: themes; stories and characters in literature.
3. Myths – drama as an aid to the understanding of myths both on an intellectual and an emotional level.
4. Poetry – drama to aid the physical appreciation of rhythm, metre and shape.
5. The Novel – drama in the appreciation of form, structure, pattern.
6. Plays: performance and the text – 'lit. crit.' and the use of improvisation acting as a means of discovering three-dimensional qualities. Communication on several levels – aural, visual, mood. Seeing the play as a unity.
7. Literature as a means of developing drama: material; ideas; methods.

JOHN HODGSON

5. *THE PROFESSIONAL THEATRE IN AND FOR SCHOOLS*

1. *Sudden acceleration of interest in recent years*
Only recently that professional repertory theatres have moved in noticeably to a field long toiled in by Caryl Jenner, Brian Way et al.

Why? Is it jumping on a bandwagon; sincerely related to the general growth of 'Drama' in schools; connected to growth of subsidies; self interest in fostering the audiences of tomorrow (and is that an illusion?), etc.?

2. *What do the professional reps do in this way?*
Test your knowledge of activities in this field by asking yourself how much you know of these kinds of activity being undertaken: tours with specially written shows into schools at all age levels;

'workshop' sessions, related to 'participation', in either a 'theatre' or 'drama' way, both in schools and in clubs and 'Saturday morning' type sessions; courses for teachers; youth theatre groups; exhibitions and talks and backstage visits; days when children come to the theatre to learn about drama in action, often related to plays they are studying or to productions in the particular theatre; professional theatre people and teachers working together to further various kinds of drama work with young people.

3. *Weaknesses of some of this work*

Lack of co-operation between theatres and teachers.

Ignorance on the part of those appointing the workers in this field as to what is really needed.

Financial instability of many schemes undertaken.

Bad organization and administration from a profession geared to 'moving on' when working with the staider and more constant machines of educational admin.

Considerable shallowness and an illusion that three visits to a school per term is something of depth. Arguably nonsense for the visitors can't possibly know the children properly.

Too much of the work seems to be a substitute, and an inadequate one, for the drama work which the schools themselves should be undertaking. Where this is the case, the work must often be carried on in a vacuum and thus diminished in value and may be accepted by educational authorities as a long term stop gap to prevent the serious employment of proper teachers.

Distrust of the work itself by many professionals. The creation of special 'teams' apparently dedicated to this work may, on the other hand, be undesirable. Their place in the professional theatre world may be a poor one, so that the best people are not available to such teams and they are regarded as a dreaded infiltration by the 'real' actors.

Lip service from all and sundry.

The fact that work undertaken in and for schools is often nullified by the general attitude and atmosphere already existing in the schools, which inhibits the work or generally shatters 'public relations' because it cuts across almost everything that the work itself stands for or is thought to be associated with.

The unwillingness of many teachers constructively to criticize the work undertaken, so that the responsibility for standards and aims is thrown back almost entirely – and dangerously – on theatre people.

General haste and lack of long term planning, which in no way stands to improve the general feeling of confusion of aim and imprecision of purpose. Hand to mouth potboiling.

MARK WOOLGAR

6. CHILDREN'S PLAY DEVELOPING INTO DRAMA

Discussion might be in the nature of a search for answers to the following four questions:

1. What are the elements in children's play that are also to be found in drama?
2. What are the elements in adult drama that are also to be found in children's play?
3. How do you recognize when dramatic play ceases to satisfy as an end in itself and becomes an activity recognizable as Drama?
4. What is the role of the teacher in helping children to get the maximum experience at each stage, and during the transition between them?

7. IMPROVISATION WITH SPECIAL REFERENCE TO GROWTH IN CHILDREN

1. Granted that growth is not an even progression but that at times the individual needs to explore both sides of the present, can spontaneous play acting enable children to:
   (a) Safely regress, and give expression to unfulfilled infantile needs.
   (b) Project themselves into their future adult roles.
   (c) Be themselves as they feel they are, rather than as others expect them to be.
   (d) Be 'supermen' and overcome difficulties and problems that in real life would be insoluble or insupportable?
2. Since a creative act contains an element of aggression, is it necessary for a child, firstly, to express his anti-social feelings in a socially acceptable medium such as drama, in order that he

can accept his own aggression, control it and use it creatively?

3. If a teacher believes that a child must accept his own aggressive feelings before he can use them creatively, how could he structure his drama work so that this necessary step in social growth takes place?

8. DRAMA IN RELATION TO THE TEACHING OF OTHER SUBJECTS

A. Preparation by group before the Conference.

Can we attempt to isolate ourselves the priorities we consider to be important in the teaching of our own subject areas? For example, where do we place such matters as these in relation to our particular subjects: growth of pupils' personality; acquisition of factual knowledge; attitudes developed by pupils towards our subject; imaginative skills; relation of our subject areas to the curriculum; decision-making by pupils; provision of open-ended situations leading to a variety of possible responses rather than one correct response? and the special subject disciplines (etc.) of my subject?

B. By the time the group meets we shall have all taken part in the general discussion on drama. Using, in part, these ideas can we investigate ways in which drama can provide an additional tool in the teaching of our subjects?

How much agreement do we share in the matter of priorities? Do our priorities relate to the general drama discussion held on Tuesday?

C. An examination of the place of drama in the subject areas in which we are concerned. Example:

1. Drama as a means of introducing and opening up a new area of study.

2. Role of drama in exploring problem areas arising in the course of a topic.

3. Drama used to pull together the threads of experience at the end of a topic.

4. Drama used to explore human problems confronting people living long ago, people living in different environments from our own, people discovering and introducing new scientific concepts to others.

5. Role playing, identification, participation.
6. Drama leading to discussion, research, and writing by pupils.

D. A more detailed investigation into the practical application of drama in the classroom related to a specific topic and subject of interest to the group.

This investigation would include a consideration of how the topic decided upon could be tackled by pupils of, say, 9–10 years; 12–13 years; 15–16 years.

9. SHOULD THERE BE A SEPARATE DRAMA DEPARTMENT IN SECONDARY SCHOOLS?

1. Can we or should we introduce another subject when disciplines are becoming integrated?
2. Drama and English consider themselves especially concerned with personal development; would a Drama specialist within the English Department or another Department suit better than a Head of Drama?
3. Does the creation of a department tend to isolate the subject concerned? cf. Art, Music.
4. Is a planned course necessary for what we hope to develop through Drama?
5. Is the conventional timetabling in secondary schools going to survive as a system anyway?
6. In the light of the other questions – should there be a separate Drama Department?

10. IMPROVISATION WITH SPECIAL REFERENCE TO SOCIAL DRAMA

1. Does drama heighten social awareness?
2. Can drama help children understand the implications of anti-social behaviour?
3. Can drama give children a deeper and more sympathetic understanding of the social problems of the under-privileged?
4. Can drama help children to solve social problems?

5. Does drama have any therapeutic value for the socially maladjusted?
6. Can drama supply the means for 'playing-out' anti-social behaviour?
7. Has 'role-playing' any value in social drama?
8. Does drama help children by giving them confidence to face the ever-growing social demands of the twentieth century?

11. ARE DRAMA AND THEATRE INCOMPATIBLE IN EDUCATION?

1. In Education is Drama synonymous with Improvisation?
2. In Education is Theatre synonymous with Performance?
3. Should Theatre be the end-product of educational drama?
4. Is educational drama complete in itself?
5. What sort of Theatre is valid in schools?
6. Is the School Play the only possible theatrical activity?

12. ACCOMMODATION AND EQUIPMENT FOR DRAMA AND THEATRE

'To be truly effective drama needs proper facilities. It requires space for movement, silence for concentration, rostra to build levels, and lighting to create atmosphere; it needs places in which to store costumes and properties; ultimately, it must have a space in which to mount a performance before an audience.' (National Association of Drama Advisers in *The Design of Drama Spaces in Secondary Schools*.)

'The small drama space (900–1500 sq. ft.) ... would have space for movement unhampered by school furniture.' N.A.D.A.
The average classroom is 600 sq. ft. and contains 35 desks and chairs.

'There should be acoustic isolation from other classes. While drama occasionally can be very noisy, silence for concentration is frequently necessary.' N.A.D.A.

Soundproofing is expensive.

'The floor must be level – a non-slip, non-light reflecting smooth surface. It must also be possible to create different levels with the help of portable rostra.' N.A.D.A.
The imagination can create its own levels.

'There should be a minimum of four spotlights and a switchboard with dimmers.' N.A.D.A.
Drama can easily become too theatrical.

'Drums and percussion instruments should be available as well as a good quality record player and tape recorder.' N.A.D.A.
Pupils can become too dependent on artificial stimuli – so can teachers!

'All drama needs is an empty space, and people with ideas to fill it.' A BRISTOL TEACHER
For further information:
The Design of Drama Spaces in Secondary Schools by N.A.D.A.
The Drama Studio by Richard Courtney, published by Pitman.
Stage Planning, Strand Electric.
Planning for New Forms of Theatre by Stephen Joseph, Strand Electric.

13. *PLAY, GAMES AND DRAMA*

1. *Introductory*
Frequent reference is made to children's 'dramatic play' and we are familiar with games which seem to enact a kind of drama. So, what is the difference, if any, between the 'dramas' played out by children in playground and street, and the 'educational drama' of the classroom? Examination of the differences and similarities might well throw some light on what is meant by that vague phrase 'educational drama'.

2. *Examination of Games*
The following games are suggested as subjects suitable for analysis into dramatic elements. Other suitable games would be welcomed.

Grandmother's Steps   Farmer may we cross the water
Roman Soldiers   Wally wally wallflower
Counting Games   Hi Jimmy Knocker
Party Songs e.g. Under- Wrestling Games (e.g. King of
neath the Spreading   the Castle)
Chestnut Tree

3. Comment on Games
Whatever dramatic elements we may decide these and other games possess, they have also one further thing in common: viz: the rules are of tremendous importance, e.g. in King of the Castle one (a) wrestles (b) according to a certain set of rules. Both elements are important. According to one report, children will spend almost as much time deciding on the rules as on the games, especially if they come from different backgrounds.

4. Examination of Customs and Pictures
Just as certain games can be looked at for dramatic content, so can certain children's customs and pictures. The following are suggested, but others are welcomed: Tippety, tippety tin; Hallowe'en customs; avoiding walking on pavement lines etc.; picture on dustcover of Lore and Language of Schoolchildren.

5. Children's play considered as improvisation
It has been noticed particularly in secondary schools, that in so-called 'drama classes' the children seemed to be playing a kind of 'make-believe' or 'let's pretend'. In this activity there is great personal enjoyment expressed in voice and movement, but it is very close to what they might be doing anyway in the playground; they tend to invent rules; they are both in it and out of it at the same time.

One is reminded of their games in which they imitate current or sometimes ballad heroes. Tensing, Hillary and Hunt were once the subject; now the astronauts. Alfred, Miss Muffet, Robin Hood, Davy Crockett also occur.

In such games they acquire skill of body, skill with mechanisms such as roller skates, skill in any preparation for adult life, exploration of their world, sensory experience (earth, sand and water games). These occur at all ages; they are self-perpetuating (though they may have local or temporary rules) and do not need the structure found in such games as Grandmother's Steps, etc.

This play is instinctive, deep rooted and absorbing, yet children can be both in and out of it, e.g. Fains ... etc. It has also such values as coming to terms with one's own feelings. All this is play, but is it drama?

6. One can quote many definitions of play and games. Are games a specially structured version of play?

7. *Our Task*
If one relies on children's love of 'play' in introducing drama to the school day, what else is added to make drama?
    If certain games, e.g. Grandmother's Steps, can become drama by adding character and situation, is this true of other games?
    Or is there something much more fundamental which must be achieved to translate 'play' into 'drama'?

BIBLIOGRAPHY:
The Lore and Language of Schoolchildren, Opie.
The many books referred to in Opie, e.g.:
Nursery Rhymes, Halliwell, etc.
Play in Childhood, Loewenfeld.
Human Growth and the Development of Personality, Kahn, pp. 94–100.

14. DRAMA IN THE PRIMARY AND MIDDLE SCHOOL

The purpose of this section of the Conference will be to examine the need for Drama activities in the Primary and Middle Schools, and to question the validity of the claims put forward by teachers who are experienced in dramatic work, and who consider it vital to the social, emotional and creative needs of their pupils.
    It is hoped that the discussion of these considerations will lead into a series of detailed expositions from the members of the Group who are involved in the use of Drama in Education, and who are committed to defending their opinions. At the same time we shall welcome those who are not in full agreement with these beliefs, or who may be sceptical of the advantages claimed by many who consider that Drama is an essential and integral part of Education.

After these preliminary discussions, the leader will ask the members of the Group to consider in depth the methods which can be used to involve children in Drama, and whether this means that all work in school should be directed towards Drama activities, or whether it is desirable to use these activities only as a base for the exploration of a wide variety of personal, intellectual and creative experiences.

Many teachers, not sure of the reasons for the current wide use of drama, are reluctant to involve themselves in its use. Perhaps they have not questioned its purposes, and find it difficult to analyse the results obtained by their more successful colleagues (by what criteria is this success judged?) Others may consider the use of Drama unsuitable for younger children, as to them it implies Theatrical presentation, a situation to be avoided at all costs. There are those who can see values in dramatic activity but are reluctant to begin, having no sets of rules or manuals of procedure to guide them.

This Group should have in mind a set of questions to stimulate ideas and to help its members reach some form of agreement.

1. Can the use of Drama in Primary and Middle Schools be justified?
2. Should it then be as essential for the teacher to use as all other subjects? Is drama a subject or a learning process? This question involves consideration of Teacher-Training.
3. How are we to involve ourselves and the children? Does the teacher impose, lead or be much more subtle in handling the Drama situation? What activities tend to stimulate Drama?
4. Can we arrive at an alternative name for Drama work? And should we want to?

15. *VOICE AND SPEECH IN DRAMA*

1. Define *Voice* and *Speech*.
2. Is Speech Training desirable?
3. Does participation in drama improve speech?
4. Should special attention be given to *speech* in drama?
5. At what age is 'theatre' (i.e. drama designed for a performance before an audience) desirable?
6. Does participation in 'theatre' demand special attention to

speech as one of the theatrical disciplines necessary for
performance before an audience?
7. What is our attitude to 'accent' (i.e. local variation in speech)?
8. What do we understand by 'elocution'?
9. What do we mean by 'good speech'?
10. Should we 'interfere' in any way with the child's habitual
(rather than 'natural') speech?
11. Does drama help those brought up on a 'restricted code' to
acquire an 'elaborate code'? (Bernstein).
12. Does disapproval of the scripted play result in denying
children some awareness of our (literary) dramatic heritage?

16. WRITING AS THE OUTCOME OF DRAMA

1. (a) *The Stimulus*
What should it seek to provoke?
(b) *The Experience*
Is the dramatic experience sufficient in itself?
(c) *The Result*
Prose?
Poetry?
Dialogue?
Is this first or second-hand experience?
2. Techniques of improving writing.
Study of texts and extracts.
3. Building a script: Should it be written? Who writes it? Who
has the final say?
To what extent should it be changed: In rehearsal? In per-
formance?
4. How else can writing be used as a result of drama lessons?

17. IMPROVISATION WITH SPECIAL REFERENCE TO PLAY PRODUCTION

1. *The Scripted Play*
(a) Does improvisation help one to explore the text on various
levels?

(b) Does it heighten appreciation of the author's skill?
(c) Does it distort the author's intention?
(d) Does it help in the establishment of mood and approach at rehearsal?
(e) Is it an aid to character-study?
(f) Is it an aid to the growth of teamwork?
(g) Is it an aid to the growth of personality?
(h) Is it essential, merely useful or inhibiting?

2. *The Improvised Play*
(a) Why make an improvised play?
(b) Should it be partially scripted, fully scripted or unscripted?
(c) How much rehearsal should it have?
(d) What controls has the director in the creation of the play?
(e) What controls has the director in actual performance?

18. *DRAMA AS A BASIC OR CURRICULUM COURSE IN COLLEGES OF EDUCATION*

When ideals have sunk to the level of practice it has become stagnation (Whitehead)

Much has been written about drama as part of the teacher's training in Colleges of Education and generalized aims have been advanced under two main headings:
(a) the development of the teacher as a person,
(b) the equipping of the teacher with some ideas about the aims and practice of drama in schools.
Many lecturers will admit to a sense of disquiet with what is being achieved and a suggested possible approach to a discussion on this subject might follow on these lines:
1. A disquiet with the present situation (a) accommodation (b) time (c) timetable structures.
2. Aims clearly defined. How can these aims be turned into objectives and made operational?
3. Are these operational objectives being reached?
4. What criteria can be developed to assess the value of the course?

5. Proposed changes to improve achievement with a definition of 'improvement'.
6. How can these changes be implemented?

SUPPLEMENT TO BOOKLET OF THEME PAPERS

ADDITIONAL TOPICS FOR DISCUSSION SUGGESTED BY CONFERENCE MEMBERS

1. The use of drama and theatre in Youth Clubs with special reference to personality and discipline.
2. Drama in Infant Schools – the foundation of the whole work!
3. Should all pupils have Drama classes? If this is not possible which ages should be given preference and and why?
4. *Masks*
    (a) Does the use of the half and full mask really lead to self discovery, or is it a dangerous emotional indulgence?
    (b) Is it an aid to building and discovering a character?
    (c) Can the mask be used as a specialized form of theatre today?
    (d) Does the mask influence and improve movement work?
    (e) Is it an aid to greater awareness and sensitivity in voice and speech in relation to character?
5. *Examinations*
    (a) Is it desirable to create a mode three or a mode one examination in C.S.E. Drama?
    (b) Should the examination be confined to 'Theatre Studies' and exclude educational drama and improvisation?
    (c) Does the existence of drama on the secondary school timetable for fourth, fifth and sixth years depend on the introduction of an examination in drama?
6. Is there a place for drama in a technical education?
7. The lack of good books of large cast plays suitable for children.
8. Drama in relation to other media e.g. film and T.V.
9. How much direction should be given to children within a drama programme?
10. Mime.
11. The use of drama in teaching English to foreigners or immigrants.

12. The therapeutic value of different forms of drama for the handicapped: e.g. puppetry, mime.
13. What should be the syllabus for drama teachers?
14. Is speech best taught by the drama teacher or the English teacher?
15. *Children's Theatre Companies*
    (*a*) Should 'good' amateur companies attempt to run these where professional theatre is non-existent?
    (*b*) Should they be plays performed by adults to children?
    (*c*) Should some children participate or does this destroy the illusion for the others?
16. Music for creative drama – mime to music – movement – electronic music – 'operas' of all kinds.
17. The problem of continuity – from primary to secondary to youth or F.E.
18. The lesson time factor in relation to large classes.
19. The purpose and possibilities of drama in the third school.
20. The place of drama in the grammar school.
21. Theatre and choice of play in the single sex school.
22. Dance Drama.
23. The National Youth Theatre and its relation to drama in schools.
24. The approach to drama in the Sixth Form – plans and aims for 16–18 year-olds.
25. Drama with handicapped children; the deaf or spastics.
26. Drama in Further Education Colleges.
27. The development of extra-curricular drama activity of the 'Link Group' type for leavers and recent pupils.
28. Should a drama course have a production of a play (or an improvisation) as its ultimate goal?
29. What qualities, knowledge and techniques should a drama teacher in school possess?

The above points were all raised by delegates on their Reply Forms and may be relevant during the discussions on Wednesday and Thursday.

Appendix III

'Guns' – *a Description*

THE PLAY, *Guns*, was devised in the summer of 1968 immediately after the death of Robert F. Kennedy. As a result of the various hypocrisies and sick jokes which accompanied this event, the people who eventually went to make up the cast were moved to express their feelings to each other. They found that in retrospect the same thing had been said after each assassination and the same thing had been done – nothing. Further research revealed many surprising and often shocking facts about the role of arms in the United States, the opposition to armament restriction and the whole problem of violence in an advanced modern society, the United States, was chosen as the place of reference for the play, not only because it was the scene of the actual assassination but also since it provided the best example of a complex society and the problems that confront such a community.

The play itself was composed in a rough form in one day. Additions were made, a definite structure was established and the first performance was given in July 1968. A discussion was held for both the cast and the audience afterwards, which the actors regarded as essential to promote direct audience participation and because the play has no real end on stage. Various comments and criticisms were noted and early this year further and final additions were made, some referring to the events of late 1968, especially the Democratic Convention in Chicago. *Guns* still remains with the intention of being not so much a play of direct social comment but more an expression of the feelings of the people involved.

PETER HEAD

Appendix IV

A Study of the English Civil War through a joint approach of History, English and Drama

THE PROJECT of work under review in this article was carried out by three forms of pupils in a mixed comprehensive school, and lasted for about one term.

I found myself in a relatively unusual situation for a Secondary teacher, because I was responsible for the English, History and Drama work of each of the forms. The pupils were in the second year and were grouped as:
(i)   a form of 'grammar ability'
(ii) a mixed ability form
(iii) a form of weak pupils.

Two interesting and educational factors were noteworthy. The first concerned the amount of time I was allotted for each form. This allocation gave me a total of seven forty-minute lesson periods a week. The second factor was the grouping of the pupils into forms of 'grammar', mixed ability and weak. This latter factor alone suggested possibilities for an experimental approach based upon some sort of comparison of the relative strengths and weaknesses of such groupings of pupils and how far these groups required completely different learning materials and methods of teaching.

I rejected the idea of keeping the three subjects of English, History and Drama in separate compartments and concentrated instead upon a topic that would bring together the essential internal coherence of these subjects. This was not difficult because all three subjects came under a 'Humanities' heading. By this I mean that the area of each subject is essentially concerned with a study of human behaviour and experience. History in schools is usually concerned with an objective study of human behaviour as revealed in the observations of how people living in other times from our own tackled the problems and difficulties dominating their generation. English and Drama are more concerned with the subjective analysis of human experience. Integrity to human experience is a core discipline. I therefore decided to embark upon a topic of study which would allow pupils to consider human behaviour not only in an objective frame of reference, but also from the viewpoint of subjective human experience.

The topic chosen for study was the English Civil War of the seventeenth century. The approach depended upon an enquiry-based form of teaching. The area of the Civil War was to be regarded as a divergent one. That is I did not intend to chart out a term's work in advance thereby encouraging convergent working, but rather than this I wanted to follow-up with the pupils aspects of the war in which they showed special interest. My approach would lead into areas where there is no simple factual correct or incorrect answer. The individual responses and judgements of the pupils would provide the basis for discussion and work. And these responses and judgements are probably of more importance educationally than the 'correct' ones which are sometimes forced upon the pupil almost without his participation in any way.

During this work Drama was regarded as an educational tool which would enable pupils, by a variety of role-playing situations, to explore material more deeply. It aided the subjective analysis of human experience. Sometimes Drama would be valuable in helping pupils to pull together the threads of what had been learned. Often a tape-recording employing Drama helped to crystallize what had been learned.

These remarks may give the reader some idea of the preliminary thinking before the project started.

I decided to introduce the project to all three forms in the same way. This was to tell them about a King who was facing a crisis in his life because of a certain Member of Parliament called John Pym. According to their abilities, each form then went to books in order to discover more about the King called Charles and the Member of Parliament called John Pym. After this research work each class was asked to suggest ways in which they thought the problem might have been tackled by the King and then by John ive study of the situation towards a subjective analysis of human

Pym. Drama was the means by which pupils clarified their thinking. Nothing clarifies more quickly opposing points of view than to place them in dramatic opposition to each other within a microcosm. At this stage of the work pupils were offering a variety of solutions to the problem of how the King would deal with Pym and his troublesome friends in Parliament. Although their solutions differed from what we believe happened in fact, I was not worried by this. Pupils were going through procedures of thinking which were important. Their thought was moving in a worthwhile direction as long as each attempt to 'solve' the King's problem led to discussion, analysis and a refinement of the central problem. We found ourselves moving from an objective study of the situation towards a subjective analysis of human experience as the pupils, through role playing, worked upon the possible thoughts and feelings of the characters in the situations – the King, his friends, John Pym and Members of Parliament. All the pupils worked in one large group. Some pupils introduced fresh creative thinking which fed and helped the rest of the group and allowed the weaker pupils to be involved without making demands upon them which, at present, they were unable to meet.

At the end of this stage of our work all three forms had developed an involvement in the King's problem. They were interested to know what really happened – as far as we know – and through exploring avenues of action which were not in fact taken by King Charles, the significance of the real events took on greater meaning. As explained earlier, the three forms taking part in this project were of different abilities. Thus their involvement and interest took different, *but equally worthwhile forms*. The able form of pupils showed special interest in the legalities of the situation and in the 'correct' ritual of events. This interest led them on to a study of documents from which historians themselves learn about events. They attempted to produce 'original sources' such as correspondence between the King and the Speaker of the House of Commons as well as private correspondence between the King and his friends. The mixed ability form were interested in the reactions of ordinary people and the drama of the King's abortive attempt to arrest Pym. They produced a tape to 'help other pupils of our age' to understand the situation. This group of pupils had been very critical of the school text books. Therefore they suggested a tape as a far more interesting way of teaching pupils than the text book. The weaker form showed far less interest in the legalities of the situations. Their interest centred around the plight of the wanted man, John Pym. They constructed group stories showing how several families living in ANY STREET might react to a fugitive from Royal justice. It is interesting to notice that the usual school text book often omits any reference to the moments of suspense and colour which may well catch the attention and interest of the weaker pupils.

From this starting point the classes went on to examine such topics as these: how people decided which side to support; problems of military occupation such as food shortages, shop-keepers' problems, lodging of enemy soldiers; the siege of Bristol as seen through the eyes of a Royalist spy; The Trial and Execution of King Charles.

The method of exploration of these topics varied according to the interests and abilities of the pupils. At one extreme the able pupils were producing documents such as speeches, sermons, pamphlets and posters using language forms similar to that of the seventeenth century. At the other extreme weaker pupils were compiling diary records of imaginary Bristolians, living in the seventeenth century, whose lives had been violently disturbed by the war. Experiments with dramatized tape material helped pupils crystallize their thinking before writing.

What seem to be the significant points emerging from the term's work?

First, I think, the confirmation that pre-planning of a term's work is more likely to prevent me from responding to the pupils' particular interests. A pre-planned course tends to direct the teacher's attention along a set course. The subjective analysis of human experience, which formed a part of this study, arose entirely out of the pupils' interests and could not have been effectively pre-planned by the teacher.

This leads me on to the second point. The area of work covered in this study overlaps the *subject* of History. The general title of Humanities is more likely to cover the wide area of exploration that the pupils dealt with during the term. A father's efforts to prevent his son from joining the Royalist Army is, I suppose, part of the subject called History. In working on this problem, however, pupils are constantly drawing upon and clarifying the question of parental authority in their own lives as teenagers in the twentieth century.

Another significant observation I would make about this work was the range of writing challenges which can be employed when pupils are developing the subjective as well as the objective study of History. Both personal and impersonal forms of writing are encountered.

Is such an approach as this a possibility for the teacher with only two History periods a week? I feel the answer is 'yes'. Clearly the area of study has to be more limited. Also it is necessary to re-examine the type of History syllabus which asks the teacher to cover five centuries of history in one school year. The problem for the teacher is one of selection – a selection of a few topics which, when examined *in depth* reveal areas of study that will illuminate an essential core or thread of the historical period. The reward I found in this method of working is that pupils see the relevance of a study of people living long ago, under some sort of stress, to their own problems and interests as young people growing up in the twentieth century.

R. VERRIER,
MONKS PARK SCHOOL

Notes on the Contributors

NIGEL DODD is Senior Lecturer in English at the College of St Matthias, Bristol. Formerly Senior English Master at Clifton College, Bristol.

WINIFRED HICKSON is Inspector of Schools for Bristol.

GAVIN BOLTON is Lecturer in Drama at the Institute of Education, University of Durham.

JOHN HODGSON is Head of Drama Studies at Bretton Hall College of Education.

DOROTHY HEATHCOTE is Lecturer in Drama at the Institute of Education, University of Newcastle-upon-Tyne.

VERONICA SHERBORNE is External Examiner for London University, Institute of Education.

JOHN HERSEE is Master in Charge of the School Theatre at Clifton College, Bristol.

MARK WOOLGAR is Staff Producer with special responsibility for schools at the Bristol Old Vic.